Teaching for Mathematical Understa

Practical ideas for outstanding primary le

Teaching for Mathematical Understanding develops the subject knowledge support and practical ideas from Tony Cotton's *Understanding and Teaching Primary Mathematics* into resources for full lessons. With an emphasis on developing outstanding lessons using a problem-solving approach, this highly practical guide is packed with activities that all trainee and practising teachers can use in the primary classroom.

Covering each area of mathematics, every activity offers helpful step-by-step guidance, including teaching and learning objectives, resources, lesson outlines, ideas for differentiation, assessment for learning and key probing questions. Also featured in this text are call-outs to the information contained on the book's companion website, a shared site with a range of relevant resources to support and consolidate your learning.

Teaching for Mathematical Understanding is an essential text for all trainee and practising teachers looking for inspiration and guidance towards outstanding mathematics teaching.

Companion website features include:

- video clips in which primary school teachers demonstrate the concepts covered in the book through teaching to a real class
- PowerPoint presentations which provide support for those using the book as part of a teacher training course
- updated weblinks to external sites with useful teaching information and resources.

Tony Cotton was previously Associate Dean and Head of Education at Leeds Metropolitan University, UK. Since 2012, he has been working as a freelance writer and education consultant. Tony has over 15 years' experience teaching maths education and 10 years' experience teaching mathematics in schools.

Routledge
Companion Websites

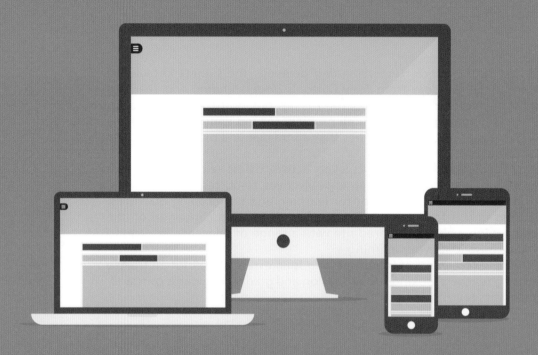

Enhancing online learning
and teaching.

www.routledge.com/cw/cotton

Teaching for Mathematical Understanding

Practical ideas for outstanding primary lessons

Tony Cotton

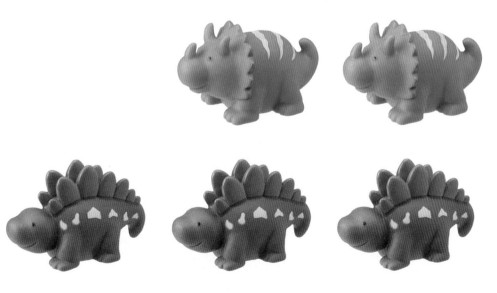

Routledge
Taylor & Francis Group

LONDON AND NEW YORK

First published 2016
by Routledge
2 Park Square, Milton Park, Abingdon, Oxon OX14 4RN

and by Routledge
711 Third Avenue, New York, NY 10017

Routledge is an imprint of the Taylor & Francis Group, an informa business

British Library Cataloguing in Publication Data
A catalogue record for this book is available from the British Library

Library of Congress Cataloging in Publication Data
A catalog record for this book has been requested

ISBN: 978-1-138-90633-4 (hbk)
ISBN: 978-1-138-90634-1 (pbk)
ISBN: 978-1-315-69555-6 (ebk)

Typeset in Frutiger
by Fish Books Ltd.

Printed by
Bell and Bain Ltd, Glasgow

CONTENTS

Acknowledgements   vi

Chapter 1   Introduction   1

Chapter 2   Learning mathematics through problem solving   7

The activities

Chapter 3   Problem solving using mathematics   13

Chapter 4   Number: Counting and place value, fractions, decimals,
            percentages and ratio and proportion   33

Chapter 5   Number: Properties of numbers   57

Chapter 6   Number: Calculating (addition, subtraction,
            multiplication, division)   75

Chapter 7   Algebra   95

Chapter 8   Geometry   113

Chapter 9   Measurement   131

Chapter 10 Statistics   153

Glossary   178
Index   181

ACKNOWLEDGEMENTS

As always I need to thank Helen for reading everything I write and trying out the ideas – my work is so much better for her input. I must also thank all the teachers and beginning teachers that I have the pleasure to work with. I learn so much from working with you and your learners. Particular thanks to Hunslet Moor Community Primary School for allowing us to film in their school for the companion website.

The last person I must thank is Felix. Felix is my grandson and I am learning a huge amount about how children learn mathematics from observing him. I also had to miss a few Fridays when I should have been looking after him to make my deadlines on this book. My apologies Felix – I'll buy you a treat out of the first royalty cheque.

CHAPTER 1
INTRODUCTION

Welcome to *Teaching for Mathematical Understanding*. I hope that the ideas in this book are exactly what I suggest in the title. I want you to find them practical – my aim is for you to think, 'I could do that in my classroom', with all of the activities. All of these activities are ones that I have used in many of the classrooms in which I have taught. I have also introduced them to trainees on teacher training courses and experienced teachers and know from their feedback that they have both found them useful and more importantly enjoyed using them. In that sense they have stood out for them from other activities – the genuine sense of 'outstanding'.

Many of you will have bought this book as a result of reading *Understanding and Teaching Primary Mathematics*, also published by Routledge. I am fortunate that this book has become very well regarded by those training to teach and teacher trainers as a useful book to develop mathematical subject knowledge. People who use the book have told me its particular strengths are that it offers practical ideas for the classroom alongside subject knowledge content and that it sees problem solving as underpinning mathematical learning. The book you are now reading develops these practical ideas into resources for full lessons. If you are reading this alongside *Understanding and Teaching Primary Mathematics* this will allow you to try out the ideas in your classroom.

The book is also designed to stand alone however. The ideas will be useful to all of you who aspire to teach lessons which bring out the best in all of your learners through developing a problem-solving approach to learning and teaching mathematics.

What makes an 'outstanding' lesson?

In 2012 Ofsted outlined what they saw as the characteristics of outstanding mathematics learning and teaching. They expected to see lessons which:

- nurtured mathematical independence and allowed learners time to think and reflect on the learning that was taking place
- were planned to include problem solving, discussion and investigation and seen as central to learning mathematics rather than an 'add on'
- saw misconceptions and errors as a step in the learning process which provided fruitful points for discussion

- allowed learners to make connections between topics and made links between mathematics, other subjects and with mathematics beyond the classroom.

You will see that the activities in this book meet these expectations. They are not designed as activities which you would use in 'special' problem-solving lessons or as one-off teaching sessions. I would hope that you would use these activities to support your day-to-day teaching of the whole mathematics curriculum. Learners who approach their mathematics as a problem-solving activity will be successful in tests as well as successful in using mathematics in their day-to-day life. This is because they see challenges and new problems as something that they can solve. They develop a resilience which means they will 'have a go'. This is a useful mind set to have when facing questions that you do not immediately know how to answer or when you cannot immediately recall the method that you have previously employed.

Why a problem-solving approach?

The section above shows that teachers who use a problem-solving approach are meeting the requirements of the English inspection regime which sees lessons which 'were planned to include problem solving, discussion and investigation' as outstanding. This view is not limited to England however. International schools which follow the Primary Years Programme are encouraged to see mathematics as a 'highly effective tool for solving problems'. The focus of the Primary Years Programme is to support learners in seeing themselves as mathematicians in the same way that we might see ourselves as 'authors' or 'artists'. I would certainly hope that by working on the activities contained in this book both you and your pupils will see yourselves as mathematicians. Real-life mathematicians spend their time problem solving – they do not fill their days completing exercises that they already know the answer to.

Another well-regarded international programme, Cambridge International Examinations, which is used in hundreds of schools around the world states that their 'curriculum is dedicated to helping schools develop learners who are confident, responsible, reflective, innovative and engaged'. They will only endorse materials which have been 'designed to engage learners in an active and creative learning journey': another piece of evidence that if we follow a problem-solving approach we are following best practice.

There is more support from the United States. Professor Jo Boaler from Stanford University has set up the largest MOOC for parents and teachers who are interested in the best way to support learners in becoming confident mathematicians. Her work can be found at http://youcubed.stanford.edu/ourmission/ and this is another rich source of materials. Jo defines mathematics as

a performance, a living act, a way of interpreting the world. Imagine music lessons in which students worked through hundreds of hours of sheet music, adjusting the notes on the page, receiving ticks and crosses from the teachers but never playing the music. Students should not be just memorising past methods: they need to engage, do, act, perform, problem solve, for if they don't use mathematics as they learn it they will find it very difficult to do so in other situations, including examinations.

(Jo Boaler, *The Elephant in the Classroom*, p30)

So – welcome to the international staff room which is the problem-solving approach to learning and teaching mathematics. It is very busy in here, but very welcoming and completely collaborative.

Which areas of mathematics do these activities cover?

As with *Understanding and Teaching Primary Mathematics* the curriculum that has been used is the most recent National Curriculum in England. However if you are working with other curriculum guidelines you will notice that there is a good match between this and other curricula and programmes of study such as the International Baccalaureate expectation for primary mathematics through its Primary Years Programme (which takes a cross-curricular approach to the curriculum) and the Cambridge Programme of Study used by many international schools around the world. This is explored in more detail in the next chapter which also unpicks the method of problem solving which underpins the approach taken throughout the book.

What do the lesson plans look like?

Each lesson – or activity (some may be more usefully explored over a series of lessons) begins with a stimulus. This may be a problem or an image which you can share with your pupils. (All these are available to download from the companion website.)

The lesson plan includes the key objectives that learners will meet as a result of working on the activity and the resources which teachers will need to have available. There are annotated lists of key vocabulary that teachers should focus on. The lesson is then outlined in detail including the way in which the teacher could introduce the session; ideas for differentiation; ways to encourage discussion whilst groups explore the activity including probing questions; and ways in which the learning can be brought together in a plenary session. Each plan also includes techniques for assessment for learning so that you and your learners know what has been learnt and the next steps in learning.

Outline of the book

The outline of the book mirrors *Understanding and Teaching Primary Mathematics* so that they are genuinely companion texts. Each 'Teaching point', 'Resource inspiration', 'Portfolio task' and 'In practice' from *Understanding and Teaching* will be developed into a classroom activity. Each activity will take the form of a lesson outline. As mentioned above, Chapter 2 outlines the approach the book takes to learning and teaching mathematics. It offers a rationale for a problem-solving approach drawing on international comparisons and recent research into effective mathematics learning and teaching. It is here that I make the links between the International Primary Years Programme and the Cambridge International Examinations programmes of study.

The following chapters take you through the curriculum. Although most activities cover more than one area of mathematics in order to support the pupils in making connections between different areas of mathematics the main focus for each chapter will be the objectives relating to the chapter's specific mathematical focus. Each chapter is structured in the same way. For example Chapter 3 takes as its focus problem solving.

Companion website

There are a series of videos available on the companion website which show young learners engaged in some of the tasks in the book. Wherever a corresponding video is available, you will see the video icon.

All the stimulus pages are available to download on the companion website should you wish to use then with your pupils. When you see this icon you will be able to download a resource sheet which pupils may need to record their responses.

You are invited to submit your children's solutions to the problems to the companion website so that you can share you solutions with a wider audience. By accessing this part of the companion website you will also be able to see how other learners in other schools have worked on the activities.

Finally the website includes a fully annotated glossary to support you in developing discussion with your pupils around key mathematical terms.

In conclusion

I hope that you enjoy using these activities in your classroom. I have found that the way I learn mathematics most effectively is to engage in tasks such as these with pupils in the classroom. They always surprise me with what they know and with what they can do. And their responses to my probing questions often give me things to think about and explore that I hadn't thought of when I was planning the session. This means that every time I teach a lesson it is different – so we can all learn (and enjoy) mathematics together.

References

Boaler, J. (2010) *The Elephant in the Classroom.* London: Souvenir Press.

Cotton, A. (2016) *Understanding and Teaching Primary Mathematics*, 3rd edition. Abingdon: Routledge.

Mason, J., Burton, L. and Stacey, K. (2010) *Thinking Mathematically.* Harlow: Prentice Hall.

CHAPTER 2
LEARNING MATHEMATICS THROUGH PROBLEM SOLVING

What is a problem-solving approach?

Can I invite you to carry out a thought experiment with me? Think of some-one you know who is good at mathematics. They can be a friend; they can be a member of your family; they might be someone you teach; they may be someone you went to school with. I want you to actually think of a person you know – not just a generic 'person who is good at mathematics'.

Now think about what it is about them that you use as evidence for thinking they are good at mathematics. What skills do they have? What aptitudes? What character traits? List them in this box

… is good at maths and they…

I have carried out this activity in over 20 different countries and I always get similar responses. The lists contain attributes such as:

- They ask interesting questions.
- They can explain themselves.
- They can carry out accurate calculations.
- They can spot number patterns.
- They like to challenge themselves.
- They don't give up if it gets difficult.
- They can see maths in everyday life.
- They make connections to maths in other subjects.
- They enjoy doing mathematics.

Can I offer you a challenge? Look at the list that you wrote in the box above. If these are the things that 'good' mathematicians do then surely we should be teaching pupils in school how to develop these skills. Think about the last lesson that you taught and highlight all of the skills in the list that you think this lesson helped your pupils develop. If there are any missing off the list think about how you might have changed the lesson to 'teach' your pupils how to be 'good' mathematicians.

I would argue that the list I shared with you above is a list of the skills that good mathematicians have. I would also argue that these are characteristics of good problem solvers. Finally I would argue that we teach these skills through working with our pupils on problem-solving activities. The activities that you find in this book will not only allow you to enjoy mathematics with your pupils, they will allow you to develop as a problem solver alongside your pupils.

In *Thinking Mathematically* John Mason argues that all pupils can be taught to think mathematically and that this is taught through practising reflection, that is by thinking carefully and by articulating how we are thinking about something. This sort of thing is best accessed and encouraged through activities which offer 'contradiction, tension and surprise'. In other words we need to be engaged in an activity which may question our current understandings if we are to 'learn' and if we are to be able to 'notice' ourselves learning.

For example – look at these three numbers

3 4 9

Which is the odd one out?
You may have said:

4 because it is the only even number

3 because it is the only prime number

3 is the only number that isn't square

9 because it is the only one bigger than 5

3 because it has five letters and the other two have four letters

These are all answers given to me by a Year 3 class last week; and all correct. At first the pupils thought that I wanted them to find just one odd one out and to guess what my reason was. Then they realised that there were lots of different answers, that any of the numbers could be the odd one out and that I didn't have an answer 'I was looking for'. Mathematics was not about guessing what is in the teacher's head but was about explaining what was in the pupil's head. This is what a problem-solving approach offers.

Another way of looking at teaching mathematics through problem solving is that it develops **relational understanding** and not simply **instrumental understanding**. The most important piece of work on this was published by Richard Skemp in 1976 in *Mathematics Teaching*, number 77, pages 20–26. This is available on the Association of Teachers of Mathematics website. His argument goes something like this:

Imagine you are exploring a park. A friend tells you paths they know to follow in the park. You walk along these paths, and quickly learn how to get from one end of this path to the other. Gradually as you explore these paths you visit new locations but if you leave any of your friend's paths you become lost. You become nervous of losing your way and never develop an overview of what the park looks like. This is **instrumental understanding**.

Instead of that you get to wander all over the park. For some parts of the park you may be guided, through other parts of the park, you explore yourself. Gradually you develop an overall picture of the park. You eventually discover the shortest paths between two points and understand the overall structure of the park. If someone shows you a new short-cut in the park you realise how this connects to the other paths you are more familiar with. You never worry about stepping off the path though, since even if you get lost, you know you will discover something interesting. This is **relational understanding**.

The activities in this book are designed to develop relational rather than instrumental understanding. The lesson plans all follow a similar pattern in order to help you overtly teach the skills of problem solving. There are four stages of solving a problem:

Represent the problem

You will be supported to work with your pupils so that they can represent the problem for themselves so that they can begin to see what they are being asked. This may be through a drawing or a diagram. They can then analyse the problem to decide what mathematics they need to use to solve the problem.

Analyse and apply the mathematics

The pupils now need to work on the problem using the mathematics that they know. You may also introduce new methods and techniques to support them. In this way they learn new mathematics in the context of a problem.

Communicate

The activities ask learners to be communicating their thinking throughout and often in presentations at the end of the process. This is through probing questions that you can use as prompts. The more you work with these activities the more asking such probing questions will become second nature.

Reflect

After each activity the pupils will be encouraged to think about 'how' they solved the problem and what they might have done differently. Reflecting on our learning makes it much more likely that we can apply it in other situations. This sort of activity means that we learn how to notice what we are doing. We stop saying that 'we just knew it' and begin to understand how we come to know things.

Chapter 1 showed that teachers across the world are embracing this approach. The English National Curriculum, the International Baccalaureate Primary Years Programme and Cambridge International Examinations all encourage teachers to develop problem-solving skills in their mathematics classrooms.

I hope that these activities show you that all of your pupils can become good mathematical thinkers and that you can become a better mathematician yourself through working on these activities with your pupils. I also argue that you can teach across the whole mathematics curriculum with the activities in this book. This means you do not have to relegate problem solving to one-off lessons on a Friday or at the end of term. It can become integral to the normal way that you teach all of mathematics.

What areas of mathematics are covered?

The book takes as its starting point the National Curriculum in England. However I work with many teachers across the world who have asked for activities which will support them in teaching the curriculum they work with. Because of this the activities are also linked to the Cambridge International Examinations programme of study which is followed by international schools in 160 countries around the world.

The curriculum in England is structured as follows:

Key stage 1

In key stage 1 (Stages 1 and 2) pupils develop confidence and mental fluency with whole numbers, counting and place value. They work with numerals, words and the four operations, including with practical resources and develop their ability to recognise, describe, draw, compare and sort different shapes and use the related vocabulary. They also describe and compare different quantities such as length, mass, capacity/volume, time and money. By the end of year 2 (Stage 2) pupils know their number bonds to 20.

Lower key stage 2

In lower key stage 2 (Stages 3 and 4) pupils become increasingly fluent with whole numbers and the four operations, including number facts and the concept of place value. This should ensure that pupils develop efficient written and mental methods and perform calculations accurately with increasingly large whole numbers.

Pupils develop their ability to solve a range of problems, including with simple fractions and decimal place value. They analyse shapes and their properties and describe the relationships between them. They are taught to use measuring instruments with accuracy and make connections between measurement and number.

By the end of Year 4, pupils should have memorised their multiplication tables up to and including the 12 times table.

Upper key stage 2

In upper key stage 2 (Stages 5 and 6) pupils extend their understanding of the number system and place value to include larger integers up to 10 000 000. This develops the connections that pupils make between multiplication and division with fractions, decimals, percentages and ratio.

Pupils are taught to solve a wider range of problems, including increasingly complex properties of numbers and arithmetic which demand efficient written and mental methods of calculation. Pupils are introduced to the language of algebra as a means for solving a variety of problems. Pupils classify shapes with increasingly complex geometric properties and they learn the vocabulary they need to describe them.

By the end of Year 6, pupils are expected to be fluent in written methods for all four operations, including long multiplication and division, and in working with fractions, decimals and percentages.

Upper key stage 2 is subdivided into the following areas:

- number: place value
- number: addition, subtraction, multiplication and division
- number: fractions, decimals, percentages
- measurement
- geometry: properties of shapes
- geometry: position and direction
- statistics.

In Year 6 (Stage 6) when 'ratio and proportion' and 'algebra' are introduced as separate areas of study.

Cambridge International Examinations programmes of study cover very similar areas of content but they are grouped slightly differently. They subdivide the content into:

- numbers and the number system
- numbers: calculation
- geometry: shapes and geometric reasoning
- geometry: position and movement
- measure

- handling data
- problem solving.

You can see immediately that 'problem solving' is a discrete set of skills to be taught here rather than assumed within the rest of the mathematics content. All the activities within this book draw on this set of problem-solving skills as I think it is important that problem-solving skills are explicitly taught rather than assumed.

As you can see there is a close match between the two curricula. To summarise, the lesson plans that follow offer you starting points linked to both the English and the Cambridge programmes of study and which:

- are accessible and extendable
- expect pupils to make decisions
- involve pupils in testing, proving, explaining, reflecting and interpreting
- promote discussion and communication
- encourage 'what if' and 'what if not' questions
- are enjoyable and contain the opportunity for surprise.

I hope you enjoy working on these activities with your learners.

Reference

Skemp, R. (1976) 'Relational understanding and instrumental understanding', *Mathematics Teaching*, 77, 20–26.

CHAPTER 3
PROBLEM SOLVING USING MATHEMATICS

The activities in this chapter will support you in developing your pupils' mathematical problem-solving skills. By working on these activities you will be able to focus on these skills. You will find that you also develop your own problem-solving skills.

Each activity is designed in the same way. On one page there is a 'task sheet' you can use with your pupils. These are available to download from the companion website. On the facing page there is a prompt sheet for you. This details:

- the target group for the task
- resources you will need
- possible starting points
- ways to represent the problem
- prompts to support you in developing mathematical thinking and reasoning: what will I need to know – which skills will I use?
- prompts to support learners in communicating their learning
- prompts for recording: things to look for and encourage
- possible developments and alternative routes through the problem
- the mathematical skills that pupils will develop whilst engaged on the task.

With all of these tasks you should have explored them yourself or with colleagues so that you feel confident working with your pupils. If you are reading or have read the companion volume *Understanding and Teaching Primary Mathematics* you may have already worked through many of these activities.

Do let yourself be surprised though – don't worry if the pupils discover things that you hadn't thought of. This is fantastic and it happens to me all the time. Similarly you will notice pupils using and developing mathematical skills that don't appear in my list.

Task 3.1 Finding 1000

Look carefully at this number grid.

1	3	5	7	…
2	6	10	14	…
4	12	20	28	…
8	24	40	56	…
…	…	…	…	…

Copy the grid down and expand it for three rows and columns.

What patterns do you notice?

Do you think every number will appear if you extend the grid far enough?

Why do you think this?

How many times will each number appear? **Once or more than once?**

Why do you think this?

Do you think 1000 will appear?

Describe its position if you think it will appear.

Target group: upper key stage 2/Stages 5 and 6.

Resources: large sheets of squared paper to make copies of and to extend the grid.

Possible starting point: ask pupils to work in pairs to discuss the patterns that they can see. Starting with this discussion avoids pupils leaping straight into 'looking for 1000' which is a temptation. Spotting the doubling patterns will help them later when they do try to find 1000. They may notice doubling, in the patterns in the numbers that you add as you move down the grid

e.g.

$+1; +3, +5: +7$

as you move down from row 1 to row 2

and patterns in the grid such as

1	3
2	6

1 + 2 + 3 = 6

and lots more!

Don't rush through this section. It gives the pupils a real 'feel' for the patterns within the grid.

Represent the problem: it is helpful for the pupils to recreate the grid. The 'copying' gives the pupils space to think and to 'notice' the patterns. This in turn enables them to notice patterns and to extend the grid.

Developing mathematical thinking and reasoning: ask the pupils 'what do you notice'? When they offer one pattern ask them to show you an example on the grid. Then ask them to find other examples in different places on the grid. For example if they notice

1	3
2	6

1 + 2 + 3 = 6

look for another 2×2 block. Say

5	7
10	14

in this case **5 + 10 + 7 = 22** (not **14**)

Why is this the case? Is the first observation true for all 2×2 blocks in the first two columns? Why? And so on.

Communicating learning: encourage pupils to explain their thinking to each other and to you throughout the task. When a pair finds a pattern in the opening of the task ask them to explain it to another pair. At several points in the lesson ask pupils to come to the front of the class and describe a pattern that they have found. At the end of the lesson ask pairs to share their 'proofs' that every number appears once and only once and that '1000' appears just once.

Recording: encourage pupils to annotate the grids with arrows showing the 'addition' from one row or one column to the next. This will help them see patterns here too.

Possible developments: pupils could design their own number grids using similar rules. What happens if we multiply by 3 as we move down the grid? What about multiplying by 4?

Other pupils may want to explore powers of 2 which appear in column 1. You could introduce problems such as the 'grain of rice problem'.

> ## Problem
>
> If a chessboard has a grain of rice placed on each square with one grain on the first square, two on the second, four on the third, and so on, how many grains of rice would be on the chessboard at the finish?

or

> ## Problem
>
> If I earn 1p on my first day at work, 2p on my second day, 4p on the third day and so on, how much would I earn in a week? In a month?

Skills developed:

- communicating their mathematical understanding
- following a specific line of enquiry explaining the choices they are making

- making well-informed decisions about the most appropriate way to represent and report their thinking
- extending their understanding of the number system to include larger integers
- doubling and halving numbers up to 100 (and beyond).

Task 3.2 Consecutive numbers

Look at the number line below.

1	2	3	4	5	6	7	8	9	10	11	12	13	14	15

Pick any two consecutive numbers and add them together.

For example

$$2 + 3 = 5 \text{ and } 8 + 9 = 17$$

What do you notice?

Does this happen for all pairs of consecutive numbers?

Why do you think this happens?

Try this with three consecutive numbers.

What about four consecutive numbers?

Target group: lower key stage 2/Stages 3 and 4.

Resources: mini whiteboards or scrap paper for developing ideas.

Possible starting point: ask pupils to work in pairs or small groups on the initial activity. Encourage them to keep trying different pairs until they notice the pattern.

(The answer is double the first number + **1.**

So **7 + 8 = 15.** Double **7 + 1)**

Represent the problem: it may be helpful to model the answer using cubes or blocks. In this way pupils can see that we are actually adding **7 + (7 + 1)** in the above example.

Developing mathematical thinking and reasoning: once pupils notice the rule for adding two consecutive numbers ask them to 'conjecture' what the rule might be for three consecutive numbers and then test it out. Again, modelling with cubes might help them think this through.

Communicating learning: when a pair is confident in their explanation for two consecutive numbers ask them to to share their 'proof' with the class. At the end of the lesson repeat this with three and four consecutive numbers.

Recording: encourage pupils to draw the blocks to help them in their generalisation.

Possible developments: the lines of development are built into the task. This can be extended to look at any number of consecutive numbers. For more experienced learners they could begin to look at algebraic representations.

$$n + (n + 1) = n + n + 1 = 2n + 1$$

(which means double the first number + **1)**

Skills developed:

- using pictures and diagrams to represent problems and organise their thinking
- identifying and explaining simple patterns involving numbers
- choosing appropriate mental strategies to carry out calculations
- investigating simple relationships between numbers
- identifying simple relationships between numbers
- knowing and using addition facts to 20 (and beyond)
- adding pairs of two-digit numbers.

Task 3.3 Odds and evens

These are even numbers.   **2, 4, 6, 8, 10**

These are odd numbers.   **1, 3, 5, 7, 9**

Pick two even numbers and add them together. Draw the answer in a grid.

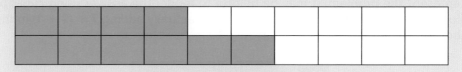

For example   **4 + 6 = 10**

Try this with other even numbers. What do you notice?

Pick an even number and an odd number. Add them together. Draw the answer in a grid.

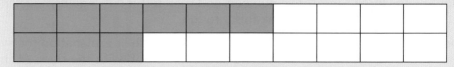

6 + 3 = 9

Try this with other even and odd numbers. What do you notice?

Pick two odd numbers and add them together.
Draw the answer in a grid.

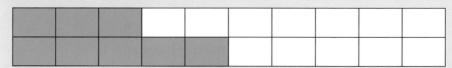

For example   **3 + 5 = 8**

What do you notice?

Target group: key stage 1/Stages 1 and 2.

Resources: cubes and squared paper.

Possible starting point: this activity is much better carried out practically rather than using any written materials. Ask pupils to work in pairs to 'build' even and odd numbers. Ask them how they remember which numbers are even and which numbers are odd. They could model this by splitting the towers into two parts. Even numbers have towers that are equal, odd numbers have towers with 'one left over'.

Then ask the pupils to explore the addition of pairs of even numbers, an odd and an even, and pairs of odd numbers.

Represent the problem: pupils can either represent the numbers by colouring in squares as on the facing page or by using cubes. For example

5 + 5 = 10

Developing mathematical thinking and reasoning: encourage pupils to articulate their thinking throughout. If they come up with a conjecture ask them to try another example to check that it is true in several cases.

Communicating learning: when pairs are confident in their explanations ask them to explain their thinking to you. They can then explain this to the rest of the class.

Recording: encourage pupils to draw the blocks after they have built the towers so that there is a record of their thinking. When they explain their thinking to you annotate their pictures so that there is a written record of their thinking.

Possible developments: some pupils could use multiplication as repeated addition to explore simple examples of

even × even
even × odd
odd × even

Skills developed:

- recognising simple patterns and talking about what they see
- talking about decisions they are making
- identifying simple relationships between numbers
- developing fluency with whole numbers while working with concrete resources
- using number facts to solve problems
- adding using concrete objects
- recognising the commutative property of addition
- recognising odd and even numbers to 20.

Task 3.4 Seating arrangements

Three friends always travel to school together and sit on the back seat of the car.

How many different ways can they sit on the seat?

Target group: key stage 1/Stages 1 and 2.

Resources: cubes of different colours and squared paper.

Possible starting point: this activity is much better carried out practically rather than using any written materials initially. One possible starting point is to get three pupils to the front sitting in three chairs to explore the problem practically. Once they can see what the problem is ask the pupils to work in groups using coloured cubes to model the problem.

Represent the problem: initially pupils represent the problem concretely. They can then use coloured cubes to begin to explore all the possibilities:

and so on.

Developing mathematical thinking and reasoning: encourage pupils to check that they have all possibilities. Can they explain how they know that they have each possibility? Ask groups to check with each other to see if they have missed any permutations. Encourage pupils to begin to work systematically. In the diagram above we fixed blue in the first position and found both the possible arrangements.

Communicating learning: when pairs are confident in their explanations ask them to explain their thinking to you. They can then explain this to the rest of the class.

Recording: encourage pupils to draw the different permutations. When they explain their thinking to you annotate their pictures so that there is a written record of their thinking.

Possible developments: it is good to move all pupils onto exploring the number of patterns with four colours as this can still be modelled (there are 24). They certainly need to be systematic for this set of permutations or they will quickly become confused.

Skills developed:

- recognising simple patterns and talking about what they see
- talking about decisions they are making
- identifying simple relationships between numbers
- exploring number patterns and puzzles
- identifying simple relationships between numbers
- explaining methods and reasoning orally.

Task 3.5 How many at school today?

This list shows the number of pupils at Cotton Academy today.

Year 1	28
Year 2	31
Year 3	25
Year 4	22
Year 5	25
Year 6	30

Work with a partner. Try to calculate the total number of pupils at school by mental addition.

Talk to your partner.

Did you get the same answer?

Tell your partner how you worked out the answer. Remember you don't have to add all the numbers up in order.

Make up problems like this for your friends to do.

You need to be able to work the answers out mentally yourself for the problem that you set.

Target group: Y3/4 Stages/3 and 4.

Resources: none necessary. You can use calculators to check the answers.

Possible starting point: the task suggests that pupils calculate this mentally and then check the answer with a partner. They should then describe their calculation strategy to their partner. Encourage pupils to estimate at first. Can they tell you a number that they know the answer will be larger than? What do they know the answer will be smaller than?

Represent the problem: pupils could annotate the task sheet to show which numbers they added. They could add arrows between 22 and 28 to make 50 and 25 and 25 to make 50. This will help them think about pairs of numbers they might use when setting their own problems.

Developing mathematical thinking and reasoning: encourage pupils to describe their calculation strategies carefully. When they are setting their own problems ask them why they are choosing particular numbers. Encourage them to think of a range of possibilities for number pairs or even triples.

Communicating learning: when pairs are confident in their explanations ask them to explain their thinking to you. The more confident pupils can then explain their calculation methods to the rest of the class.

Recording: when pupils are solving the problems ask them to describe their strategies to you. They can then either annotate the grids themselves or you can annotate them. Display the problems so that the pupils can see all the different problems that have been set and the strategies for solving them.

Possible developments: you could work with two groups in each year. Let the pupils set the problems themselves and encourage them to be as challenging as they feel able. You can also use the real data from your school on a day-to-day basis as this will encourage them to repeat strategies that have been successful.

Skills developed:

- checking the reasonableness of an answer
- making well-informed decisions about the strategies they should use
- identifying patterns that will help solve a problem
- adding pairs of two-digit numbers
- understanding that addition is commutative
- choosing appropriate mental strategies to carry out calculations
- making a sensible estimate of an answer.

Task 3.6 Domino totals

Play a game of dominoes – can you make a total of 6 each time?
Can you use all the dominoes?

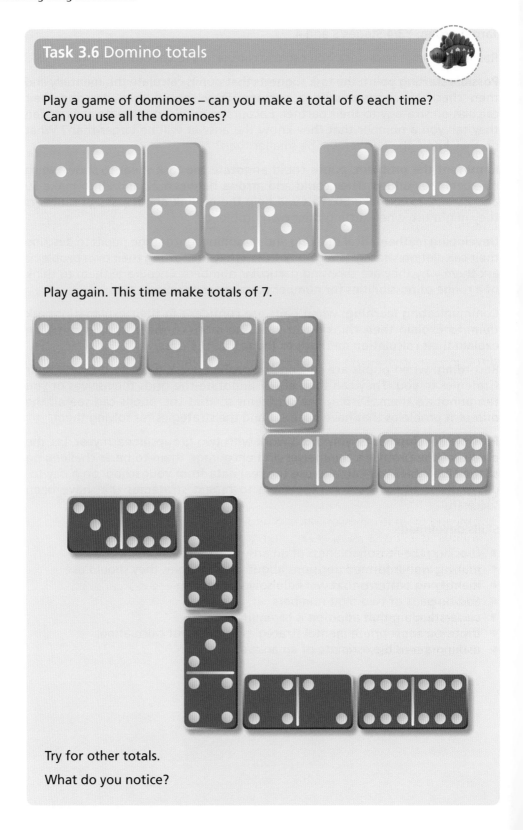

Play again. This time make totals of 7.

Try for other totals.

What do you notice?

Target group: Y3/4/Stages 3 and 4.

Resources: sets of dominoes. Enough sets for small groups to work on the task.

Possible starting point: you may need to introduce the rules of dominoes. Play a few ordinary games first if pupils are unused to them. Look at the totals that are being made where the dominoes join. Then set up the task to make totals to 6.

Represent the problem: pupils may find it helpful to list all the possible dominoes at some point so that they have a list to use. Other pupils may choose to use the dominoes themselves to represent the problem.

Developing mathematical thinking and reasoning: encourage the pupils to try alternative arrangements. They may feel as though they should just try one arrangement. They need to explore several possible arrangements. The final question in the task is the key to digging deeper into the mathematics. Encourage them to describe their findings in as much detail as they can. Asking 'why' and 'what if' questions at this point is important. Are there totals which are impossible? Can they convince you?

Communicating learning: pupils should describe what they are finding to you orally at first. They can refine these arguments through talking to you and through your questioning. Once they have a succinct argument encourage them to write it down, or write it down for them.

Recording: pupils may find it useful to note all the possible arrangements. They may also need to sketch examples using images of dominoes.

Possible developments: encourage pupils to come up with their own ideas for extensions as a first option. You could explore what would happen if you had a set of dominoes up to 7 or 8 etc.

Skills developed:

- drawing on mathematical skills to undertake an investigation
- following a line of enquiry explaining the choices they are making
- looking for patterns
- identifying simple relationships between numbers
- making well-informed decisions about how to represent and report thinking
- suggesting a range of possible lines of enquiry
- investigating a simple general statement
- using ordered lists and tables to solve problems.

Task 3.7 Pentominoes

How many different ways can you arrange five squares so that two sides touch exactly?

How can you be sure you have all the different arrangements?

Which of the nets will fold to make an open cube?

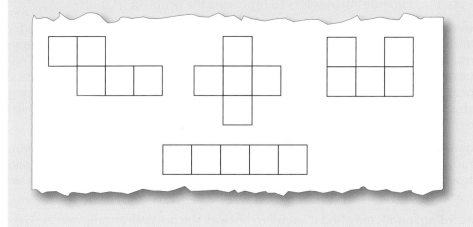

Target group: Y3/4.

Resources: squared paper; square templates; scissors.

Possible starting point: allow pupils to explore the task using the task sheet as a starting point. It may be appropriate for pupils to look at simpler cases when they are trying to find out if they have all possibilities. The simplest case would be two squares for which there is only one possibility. Then try three and four.

Represent the problem: pupils can sketch their pentominoes on squared paper. Ask them to think about ways that they can 'classify' the pentominoes.

Developing mathematical thinking and reasoning: pupils need to decide what they are counting as 'different'. It is helpful to see rotations as the same. You can illustrate this using the case of two squares. So they are the same.

Communicating learning: pupils should describe the criteria they are using to classify the pentominoes. This becomes important when they are checking they have all the possible arrangements. They should articulate their reasoning to convince you that they have all possibilities. Try to avoid giving an 'answer' at this point. They should reach a stage when they know that they have all the possibilities rather than check with you that they have them all. (There are 12 distinct arrangements.)

Recording: pupils need to sketch all the possible arrangements. They may find it useful to organise this recording systematically.

Possible developments: begin to explore the possibilities with six squares folding into a cube. You could also explore possibilities with equilateral triangles.

Skills developed:

- drawing on mathematical skills to undertake an investigation
- following a line of enquiry explaining the choices they are making
- using mathematical reasoning to analyse shapes and describe the relationships between them
- making well-informed decisions about how to represent and report thinking
- suggesting a range of possible lines of enquiry
- investigating a simple general statement
- using ordered lists and tables to solve problems.

Task 3.8 A sustainable school

How sustainable is your school?

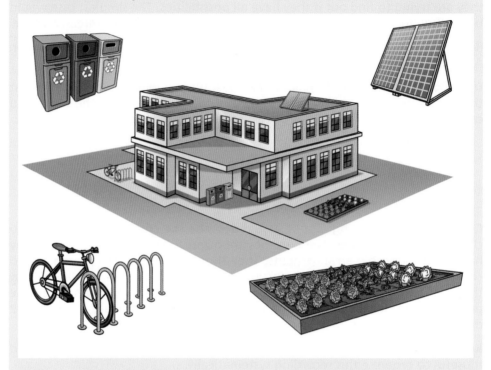

What could you do to find out?

What changes could you make as a result of your research?

Prepare a report for the school council which recommends changes and gives the reasons for these changes.

Target group: Y5/6.

Resources: this project will develop over several lessons. Respond to the pupils' needs to allow them to have the resources they require.

Possible starting points: the most effective way to begin such a project is to ask your pupils how they could explore this issue. Do some research for yourself first. How much waste paper is thrown away each day? How much does the school spend on paper and photocopying? What are the annual fuel bills? What are the implications for pollution for the ways that pupils travel to school? Some of the areas which learners have explored with me on this extended project over the years have included the following:

- Car parking
  What is the most effective way of redesigning the car park so that it uses a minimum of space and so that it can incorporate a bike shed to encourage cycling to school? This involves measurements of cars, the construction of scale models and trying out different arrangements for parking spaces. The issue of ensuring there are sufficient parking spaces for those needing accessible parking is also important.

- Travel to school
  My pupils have always enjoyed surveying the whole school to find out how teachers and pupils get to school. They can then calculate the current carbon footprint. This has led to pupils exploring ways of lift sharing, of walking buses, of cycling schemes where pupils meet up and cycle to school together. The mathematics involved also involves exploring shortest routes to school, and possible 'pick-up' points.

- Recycling paper
  Again, a brief survey can ascertain which classes use most paper; which classes are best at recycling paper and the money that can be saved through recycling paper internally as scrap paper, or in home-made exercise books. A trip to the recycling plant is always popular.

- Energy bills
  Sharing the energy costs within a school has always led to pupils becoming incredibly vigilant about turning off lights and thinking carefully about energy usage. In two schools I have worked in they have offered the school council a share of any money saved through cutting energy costs and the school council has been able to make the decision about how they will spend this money.

Represent the problem: this will vary depending on the choices pupils make. Encourage them to record their findings carefully, first in draft form and then in neater versions so they can build the records into the presentations.

Developing mathematical thinking and reasoning: ask 'why' and 'what if' questions throughout the process. Ask pupils to explain the choices they are making and to convince you that their conclusions are accurate.

Communicating learning and recording: pupils should prepare a presentation that they give either to the rest of the class or to the school council or head teacher. This gives a real purpose to the project.

Possible developments: pupils will have other interests which they could explore using mathematics. There may be school twinning projects and you could explore similarities and differences between the experiences of the pupils in the twin schools for example.

Skills developed: this will depend on the choices the pupils make. Use the programme of study with the pupils at the end of the project and ask the pupils to audit the skills that they have been using and developing.

CHAPTER 4

NUMBER Counting and place value, fractions, decimals, percentages and ratio and proportion

These activities develop some of the tasks and 'resource inspiration' ideas in the companion volume to this book, *Understanding and Teaching Primary Mathematics*. The 'big ideas' covered in the chapter are:

- counting
- place value
- fractions, decimals and percentages
- ratio and proportion.

The activities in this chapter will support you in developing your pupils' mathematical skills in counting and understanding number. By working alongside them you will also develop your own mathematical skills in this area.

Each activity is designed in the same way. On one page there is a 'task sheet' you can use with your pupils. These are available to download from the companion website. On the facing page there is a prompt sheet for you. This details:

- the target group for the task
- resources you will need
- possible starting points
- ways to represent the problem
- prompts to support you in **developing mathematical thinking and reasoning:** what will I need to know – which skills will I use
- prompts to support learners in communicating their learning
- prompts for recording: things to look for and encourage
- possible developments and alternative routes through the problem
- the mathematical skills that pupils will develop whilst engaged on the task.

With all of these tasks you should have explored them yourself or with colleagues so that you feel confident working with your pupils. If you are reading or have read the companion volume *Understanding and Teaching Primary Mathematics* you may have already worked through many of these activities.

Do let yourself be surprised though – don't worry if the pupils discover things that you hadn't thought of. This is fantastic and it happens to me all the time. Similarly you will notice pupils using and developing mathematical skills that don't appear in my list.

Task 4.1 Estimating cubes

This is a game for four people.

You need about 15 small cubes or other small objects and a shallow container. You also need a piece of card you can use to cover the container.

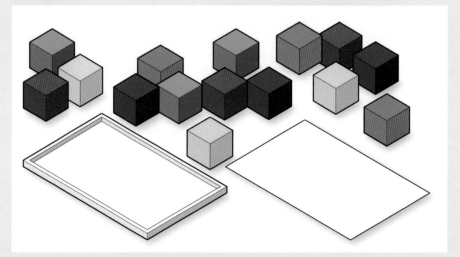

One person picks up a handful of the cubes without counting. Drop the cubes into the container. Count to three and then cover the container. The others in the group should estimate how many cubes there are. Do not allow time to count.

Each person then says how many cubes they think there are and describes how they estimated.

What is the largest number that you got correct?

Draw the different ways that you tried to group the cubes to estimate.

Did you get better the more times you played the game?

Target group: Y1/2/Stages 1 and 2.

Resources: cubes or other small objects; shallow container; piece of A4 card to cover the container.

Possible starting point: you could model the activity with the whole group. Sit the pupils in a circle around a table or on the carpet and throw the cubes. Cover them quickly with a cloth. Pupils could discuss with a partner how they grouped the cubes to 'count' them.

For example in the image above they may see two blue bears and four other bears and so know there are six.

Represent the problem: encourage the pupils to sketch their answers and draw a line around the groups. In the example above they could represent the bears by crosses or dots and would have one group of four and another of two. Pupils could record this as a number sentence if they have been introduced to formal recording.

Developing mathematical thinking and reasoning: this develops pupils' 'number sense' by encouraging them to see patterns within numbers. In the above example they are seeing 6 as 4 + 2 and 2 + 4. Given the same arrangement other pupils may have seen 6 = 3 + 3. It is important to explore all the different groups that pupils see.

Communicating learning: pupils should be encouraged to discuss all the ways that they are seeing the number and realise that there is not a single way to group the objects. Through this discussion they will see that the larger groups they can operate with the better their chance of estimating close to the number.

Recording: encourage learners to draw what they are visualising, drawing lines round the groups and recording a number sentence underneath or simply the total if they have not been introduced to formal recording at this stage.

Possible developments: learners could find all possible pairs to make particular totals.

Skills developed:

- reading and writing numerals from 0–20
- counting in steps of 2, 3 and 5
- giving a sensible estimate of objects
- representing and using number bonds to 20
- understanding addition as combining sets
- using + and = signs to record addition.

Task 4.2 Counting on a number track

Lay out the number tiles in order.

You need two foam dice – one red and one blue.

Roll the blue dice and hop that number forward. Roll the blue dice again and hop forward. Now roll the two dice together. Move forward the number shown on the blue dice and back the number shown on the red dice.

You win if you get past 20.

You lose if you go back past 0.

What is the least number of turns you took to win?

What is the least number of turns you took to lose?

Target group: Y1/2/Stages 1 and 2.

Resources: carpet tiles from 0–20 to make a number track; two large foam dice in different colours.

Possible starting point: this should be a game that pupils keep returning to and can play whenever they choose. Keep the tiles and the dice in an easily accessible place so that pupils can set the game out for themselves. You may want to play the game a few times at the beginning of sessions so that the pupils get used to the 'rules'.

Represent the problem: at this stage it is the discussion and the use of language that is important. Representing the movement on paper is not a key focus for this activity. Some pupils may be able to represent the moves on a paper-based number track. They could move on to playing a similar game with small dice on a number track on a board.

Developing mathematical thinking and reasoning: play the game with the pupils and ask them questions to 'help you'. Say things like 'I have thrown a 4 on the blue dice – what should I do?' And ask pupils to predict after they have thrown a number, saying 'Which square do you think you will land on?'

Communicating learning: play the game with the pupils and model mathematical language for the pupils. You can use phrases such as 'I moved on three spaces from 5 to 8. So 5 plus 3 is 8' and so on.

Recording: it may be appropriate to record some of the moves on a number line although this should only be at a point where the pupils are playing the game confidently. Some pupils could also record on a number line using an arrow and then write the appropriate number sentence.

Possible developments: play similar games on a number line using smaller dice.

Skills developed:

- reading and writing numerals from 0–20
- counting in steps of 2, 3 and 5
- understanding addition as combining sets
- using + and = signs to record addition.

Task 4.3 Measuring temperature

Use the web to find information about temperatures in different countries.

Show this information on a table and on thermometers.

Jan	Feb	Mar	Apr	May	Jun	Jul	Aug	Sep	Oct	Nov	Dec
−2	−5	3	5	8	10	13	18	12	17	7	−8

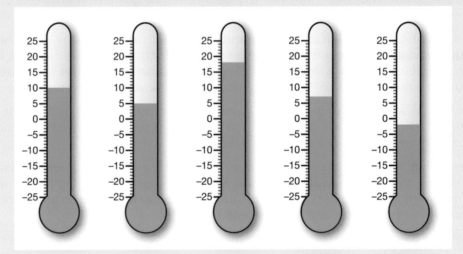

Make up five questions based on these thermometers to ask your friends. Remember you must be able to work out the answer yourself.

Target group: Y5/6/Stages 5 and 6.

Resources: access to web so pupils can carry out research; blank copies of thermometers. (These are available on the companion website.)

Possible starting point: Ask pupils to work in talk partners to match the thermometers to the temperatures. Ask the pupils if they can think of any other real contexts when directed numbers are used (money/golf scores) and introduce/remind them of the vocabulary of positive and negative numbers. Model a question that they might ask: 'How much hotter is it in March than February?' for example. Again, ask pupils to calculate this using talk partners. Ask for answers and strategies – if pupils do not demonstrate the use of the thermometer as a number line show them how they could do this.

Represent the problem: pupils should use the blank thermometers as number lines for their own questions. They could then move on to a horizontal number line marked from –20 to +20.

Developing mathematical thinking and reasoning: the use of talk partners to explore this area is important so that pupils can construct their own meanings. As is the use of a real context. Encourage pupils to ask a range of questions. They should find the differences between temperatures and ask how much hotter (addition) and how much colder (subtraction) questions. You can then show them that 'addition' involves moving to the right on a number line and 'subtraction' involves moving to the left.

Communicating learning: ask pupils to share their questions and compare the strategies that they used to carry out the calculation. Encourage them to 'notice' the different strategies that they use for the different types of question.

Recording: pupils can move from using the template thermometers to using a horizontal –20 to +20 number line.

Possible developments: pupils could pose each other questions in different real-life contexts.

Skills developed:

- ordering and comparing numbers with one or two decimal numbers on a number line and a temperature scale
- calculating a rise and fall in temperature
- understanding everyday systems of measurement including temperature
- using negative numbers in context and calculating intervals across zero.

Task 4.4 Number sequencing

Properties of number and number sequences.

You will need:

- Cards with numbers 1–20.
- Cards with numbers 10–20.

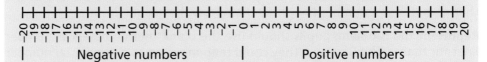

Negative numbers   Positive numbers

You will be creating number sequences with seven numbers.

- Pick a card between 1 and 20 to get the size of the steps.
- Pick a card between 10 and 20 to get the starting number.

The starting number is always the **fourth** number in the sequence.

Step size 12

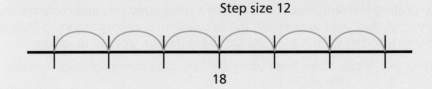

18

I picked a card. The step size is 12.

I picked a card. The fourth number is 18.

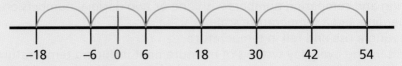

| −18 | −6 | 0 | 6 | 18 | 30 | 42 | 54 |

You might find it helpful to mark zero to remind you when you move into negative numbers.

Target group: Y5/6/Stages 5 and 6.

Resources: set of digit cards from 1–20. Set of blank number lines from –20 to + 20.

Possible starting point: draw a large number line on the whiteboard and ask a pupil to come to the front of the class. Model the activity with this pupil and a large set of digit cards. Ask pupils to work in talk partners to tell the pupil where to place the starting number and then other pupils can come to the front to draw the number sequences on the board. Record the number sequence in ascending order once it is completed. Remind the pupils of the vocabulary of positive and negative numbers.

Represent the problem: pupils should use the blank number lines to represent the numbers and record the number sequences in ascending order once they are completed. They may need to extend the number lines for some of the sequences.

Developing mathematical thinking and reasoning: the use of talk partners to explore this area is important so that pupils can construct their own meanings, as is the use of a real context. Allow the pupils to extend the number lines drawing on their own experience. They will realise that the number lines could be extended to infinity in both directions

Communicating learning: ask pupils to share their questions and compare the strategies that they used to find the number sequences. Encourage them to 'notice' the different strategies that they use for the different types of question.

Recording: they can draw their own number lines rather than relying on the printed number lines.

Possible developments: use a wider range of number cards and extend the number sequences beyond +20 and below –20.

Skills developed:

- ordering and comparing directed numbers on a number line
- using negative numbers in context and calculating intervals across zero.

Task 4.5 Place value

You need a set of digit cards from 0–9.

Pick four different digit cards.

0 1 2 3 4
5 6 7 8 9

- What is the largest number you can make with these digit cards?
- What is the smallest number?
- Make four numbers that are in between the smallest and the largest number.
- Write them in ascending order.
- Write four different number sentences using the < or > signs.
- Read these number sentences to your partner, saying the numbers aloud.

Target group: Y3/4/Stages 3 and 4.

Resources: set of 0–9 digit cards; place value cards.

Possible starting point: ask all the pupils to write _ _ _ _ on a mini whiteboard. Tell them that they you are going to roll a dice and that they have to decide where to write the number that you roll. They are trying to make the largest number they can but must place the number on the grid when you have rolled it. Once they place it they cannot move it. (They should realise that they need to place the larger numbers to the left where they have most value.) Pupils should play in pairs or small groups to encourage discussion. Repeat the game several times and alternate between making the largest and the smallest number. If a zero doesn't appear after three games make sure it does in the next game to deal with this possibility later.
 Ask pupils to say the numbers aloud to each other.

Represent the problem: ask pupils to use place value cards to make the numbers they create. This will help them when they need to say the numbers aloud.

Developing mathematical thinking and reasoning: ask pupils to explain the decisions that they are making. Why does a number have greater value in the 'thousands' column than the 'one' column?

Communicating learning: at the end of the lesson find out the largest number anyone in the class created. Ask which numbers were hardest to 'say' aloud. These will probably be numbers which included a zero such as 2043. Use place value cards to show that this is 'two thousand and forty-three' for example.

Recording: pupils should write number sentences using < and > signs. Ask the pupils to read these to you so that they get used to 'reading' mathematical sentences.

Possible developments: increase to five and six digits.

Skills developed:

- recognising place value in four-/five-digit numbers
- comparing and ordering numbers up to 10 000
- reading and writing numerals up 10 000 in numerals and words
- partitioning into thousands, hundreds, tens and ones.

Task 4.6 Multiplying and dividing by 10

1   Write a single digit in the middle of a page.

2   Multiply this number by 10 and write this number above the first number. Repeat working up the page, until you have five numbers.

3   a   Now divide your original number by 10. Write the new number below your original number.

    b   Repeat, working down the page. What patterns can you see?

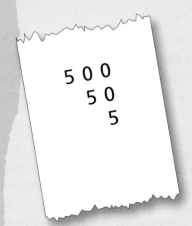

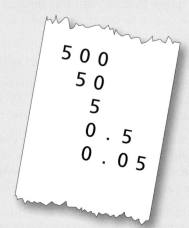

4   What happens when you divide a whole number with up to four digits by 10 and then multiply the answer by 100?

Target group: Y3/4/Stages 3 and 4.

Resources: calculators; large sheets of paper; place value grids from 'thousands' to 'hundredths'.

Thousands	Hundreds	Tens	Ones	Decimal Point	Tenths	Hundredths

Possible starting point: it is helpful to ask the pupils to carry out this activity in small groups rather than modelling it for all at the beginning. In this way they notice the patterns for themselves.

Represent the problem: once they have carried out the activity on a large sheet of paper they should transfer the list of numbers onto the place value grid so that they can see what each digit represents.

Developing mathematical thinking and reasoning: ask pupils where they have seen two places of decimals before. They will certainly recognise 'money' and some may think about different forms of measurement.

Communicating learning: ask pupils to describe what they notice. The point of the activity is to realise that the numbers are moving to the left or right across the decimal point (we are not adding zeros!). If pupils suggest the rule 'add a zero' point out that this doesn't work for decimals. You could use money as an example.

Ten times £1.50 is not £1.500.

Recording: if pupils start to draw their own place value grids this helps them visualise these grids later when exploring place value.

Possible developments: this can be extended as far as is sensible for the groups that you are working with.

Skills developed:

- recognising place value of each digit in four-digit numbers
- recognising and writing decimal equivalents of any number of tenths or hundredths
- finding the effect of dividing numbers by 10 or 100
- understanding decimal notation for tenths and hundredths.

Task 4.7 Rounding

1 When I round to the nearest 10 I get an answer of 130. What are four possible numbers that I might have started with?

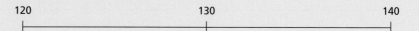

2 Whe I round to the nearest 1000 I get an answer of 12 000. Write down five possible numbers I could have started with and place them on the number line below.

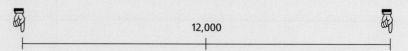

3 When I round to the nearest tenth I get an answer of 4.7. Write down six possible numbers I could have started with and place them on the number line below.

Make up similar questions of your own for your friends.

Remember you have to know whether the answer they come up with is correct or not!

Target group: Y3/4/Stages 3 and 4.

Resources: squared paper is probably best for the pupils to construct their own number lines.

Possible starting point: use a counting stick.

As a class, count along the counting stick from zero in 10s, then 100s, then 1000s. Then say that one end is 250. If you count on in 1s what would the other end be? What about the middle?

Use this to explore rounding to the nearest 10 as in the first example.

Pupils should work in pairs or small groups on the activity to encourage discussion.

Represent the problem: pupils could use mini counting sticks to help them and then use empty number lines. They need to decide what the end points and mid point will be.

Developing mathematical thinking and reasoning: encourage pupils to look for the 'numbers in between' the divisions. There are actually an infinite number of numbers between each division however small the division! Ask questions like 'what would be the smallest number that would round up to ….' and 'what would be the largest number that would round down to….?' The problem-posing activities also help develop mathematical thinking as deeper understanding is required to pose questions and to explain why answers are correct than to simply answer questions that someone else has set.

Communicating learning: pupils should explain their thinking to each other and to you. Using the probing questions above will also help pupils explain their thinking and so come to a deeper understanding.

Recording: it is helpful to record this on large sheets of paper so that pupils can get a sense of the relative size of the numbers.

Possible developments: this activity can be developed for all rounding and estimating activities. The margins of accuracy can be as small or as large as required.

Skills developed:

- rounding any number to the nearest 10, 100 or 1000
- positioning accurately and estimating where three- and four-digit numbers lie on empty number lines
- comparing pairs of three- and four-digit numbers.

Task 4.8 Fractions

Ten pupils are going to stand behind the chairs one at a time.

Once they have decided where they will stand they must stay there.

When they are all standing behind the chairs the pupils behind that chair share the chocolate in the chair.

Where should pupils stand so that they divide the chocolate up in as fair a way as possible?

Target group: Y3/4/Stages 3 and 4.

Resources: six bars of chocolate; three chairs, large sheets of paper for groups to model 'strategies' and 'solutions'.

Possible starting point: this activity should be carried out practically. Ideally group the pupils into five groups. Each group chooses two representatives to carry out the activity. At first ask the pupils to maximise the amount of chocolate they should take back to their group. Play the game once and then the pupils should return to their groups to decide on a strategy for the next round after which the chocolate will be divided up. Decide on the order in which pupils take their places behind the chairs by allocating a place in the 'queue'. You can use 1–10 digit cards for this.

Represent the problem: encourage pupils to sketch the bars of chocolate so that they can 'shade' the fractions that they will receive. Some pupils will work in decimals (as there are ten people altogether). Some will use fractions by shading.

Developing mathematical thinking and reasoning: the different possible choices that pupils make encourage them to explore fractions and decimals. Question the pupils throughout about their strategy to encourage them to articulate their thinking.

Communicating learning: encourage pupils to explain the reasons for the choices that they are making. Once the groups have decided on the 'fairest way' to allocate the chocolate ask each group to explain. The whole class can then agree on what would be the fairest distribution. I have come across lots of interesting interpretations of this when using this activity.

Recording: pupils should record informally at first to get an understanding of the problem. Encourage them to record a more 'formal' solution in their books for the final question. Say that this should be able to be understood by someone who hasn't carried out the activity.

Possible developments: pupils could explore similar problems using different numbers of pupils or bars divided into different numbers of chunks. Is the 'fairest' solution always applicable?

Skills developed:

- recognising and showing using diagrams of equivalent fractions
- solving problems involving fractions
- recognising and writing decimal equivalents of tenths
- ordering and comparing two or more fractions
- finding halves, quarters and thirds of shapes and numbers.

Task 4.9 Fractions and decimals

1   Look carefully at the pegs on the washing line. Estimate which fractions they could represent. Copy the numbers onto a large sheet of paper. Label the points A to H with their fractions and equivalent decimals.

2   Working with your partner, look at the gap between peg B and peg C. Think of a fraction that will hang on the line in the gap. Predict where it will hang. Calculate the decimal fraction to check it will fit before you hang it on the line.

3   Find a fraction to hang in each gap between pairs of letters. Remember to calculate the decimal equivalent before you add it on the line.

4   Look at the gaps between the pegs. Now find a space to add three more fractions that have a different denominator to any that are already on the line.

Target group: Y5/6/Stages 5 and 6.

Resources: large piece of string across the front of the classroom with labels pegged to the string as on the illustration; large sheets of paper for pupils to create their own 'washing lines'.

Possible starting point: recreate the image on the pupil task sheet at the front of the classroom. Ask pupils in pairs to create any image they like which represents 1/2. They may choose to draw shapes and shade a half. Some may know that 1/2 is also 50%. Select another fraction on the line to work on as a whole class. For example 'F' represents 3/4. Repeat the process for this fraction.

Represent the problem: pupils need to recreate the number line on a large piece of paper. There may be some discussion about the number of divisions needed. If they choose to divide it into tenths then 1/4 and 3/4 will fall between divisions. (This is not a problem and illustrates the fact that 3/4 falls between 7/10 and 8/10 or 0.7 and 0.8. It is a useful image for the equivalence of 3/4 to 0.75.)

Developing mathematical thinking and reasoning: ask pupils to justify the choices they make for the divisions that they choose. Compare the images that pupils are using for equivalence. It is helpful to get groups to describe their images to other groups to encourage a wide range of images. Ask pupils for a different range of images – for example there are several ways to show 3/4 as an area of a square or rectangle.

Communicating learning: use the word 'equivalent' to support pupils in developing their vocabulary. Ask pupils to present their solutions to each other in a plenary session. They should explain which fractions they did first and which they found more difficult. How did they resolve these difficulties?

Recording: the large sheets of paper are useful and should be used for display so that pupils can see the others' interpretations of the task. Pupils can also label the divisions on the number lines. For example some may label the line in tenths. This helps them see both equivalence and understand place value when they are ordering fractions with different denominators.

Possible developments: pupils can write equivalent fractions using their number lines. They could also go on to explore fraction walls to look for other equivalent fractions.

Skills developed:

- comparing and ordering fractions
- expressing halves and tenths as percentages
- recognising equivalence between fractional and decimal forms
- recognising equivalent fractions.

Task 4.10 Conversions

This table helps you convert between pounds Sterling and Euros. Work with a partner to complete the tables.

Pounds sterling	1	2	3	4	5	10	20	50	100
Euros	1.25								

What was your strategy for completing the table?

This table helps you convert from Euros to pounds Sterling.

Euros	1	2	3	4	5	10	20	50	100
Pounds sterling	0.8								

Use the same strategy to complete this table.

Five miles is approximately eight kilometres.

Draw a conversion table below using this information.

Miles	1	2	3	4	5	10	20	50	100
Km									

Write five questions for your friends that use this information.

Target group: Y5/6.

Resources: mini whiteboards for 'rough' working.

Possible starting point: it is useful to ask pupils to work on this in small groups or with partners before a whole class introduction. This allows them to develop their own strategies. Ask pairs to check with each other when they complete the first table, both to check the answers and to compare strategies. At this point hold a plenary to compare strategies and discuss which strategies are the most 'efficient and effective'. Remember a strategy is only effective if it gets the correct answer!

Represent the problem: encourage pupils to draw the tables accurately as this is helpful when they use them to work out the answers to the problems later.

Developing mathematical thinking and reasoning: sharing the strategies for completing the tables supports the development of mathematical reasoning as does comparing strategies. Explore the patterns in the tables – particularly doubles and multiples of 10. When pupils pose problems later in the session encourage them to ask questions which require pupils to combine answers. So they could find 253 Euros in pounds by doubling the 100s column and then adding 50 and 3. The problem-posing part of the session is vital to develop reasoning.

Communicating learning: ask pupils to explain their strategies for answering the questions that are posed by their friends. Pupils should work in pairs or small groups so they get used to articulating their thinking and explaining why their calculations are correct.

Recording: encourage pupils to record their calculations in full. Explain that this is so someone else could see how they have calculated the answer.

Possible developments: use a wide range of conversion tables to explore similar problems. You can often set these in real-world contexts.

Skills developed:

- solving problems involving the relative sizes of quantities
- understanding and using approximate equivalences
- using ordered lists and tables to solve problems.

Task 4.11 Cross-curricular project – planning a party

Plan a celebration party for your class.

You need to decide:

- Will the party have a theme?
  How can you decide on a good theme?
- What decorations will you need?
  How much will these cost or will you make them?
- What refreshments will you need?
  How much food and drink will you need?
- What entertainment will you provide?
- How can you make sure that the party will be the best for your class?

Target group: Y3/4/Stages 3 and 4.

Resources: this project will develop over several lessons. Respond to the pupils' needs to ensure they have the resources they want.

Possible starting point: decide on a reason for a party. This may be a celebration or you could put on a party to raise money for a charity. Children should work in groups to come up with ideas. You could then form groups which would work on different aspects of the party. For example

- Marketing group: they will advertise the party.
- Purchasing group: they will make all the purchasing decisions based on information from the decorations, refreshments and entertainment groups.
- Decorations group: they will plan and organise the decorations for the party.
- Refreshments group: they will make the decisions about refreshments including deciding how much food and drink will be needed.
- Entertainment group: they will organise the entertainment for the party.

Represent the problem: each group will need to come up with an initial plan based on some data collection for their group. This can be shared with the whole class before moving forward. Organise regular 'board meetings' at which the groups present their current plans. These presentations should include 'hand outs' or PowerPoint slides.

Developing mathematical thinking and reasoning: ask 'why' and 'what if' questions throughout the process. Ask pupils to explain the choices they are making and to convince you that their presentations are accurate and appropriate. Encourage the pupils to ask 'why' and 'what if' questions too at the 'board meetings'.

Recording and communicating learning: you could keep 'minutes' of the board meetings to encourage recording and communicating learning. It may be appropriate to ask the groups to report to the school council or to the head teacher too.

Possible developments: I know of several schools where classes run healthy tuck shops or even community lunches for local community members and parents. This sort of mini business offers lots of opportunities to develop mathematical skills.

Skills developed: this will depend on the choices the pupils make. Use the programme of study with the pupils at the end of the project and ask the pupils to audit the skills that they have been using and developing.

CHAPTER 5

NUMBER Properties of numbers

These activities develop some of the tasks and resource ideas in *Under-standing and Teaching Primary Mathematics*, the companion volume to this book. The activities in this chapter focus on properties of numbers. The big ideas underpinning all the activities covered are:

- exploring number patterns
- discovering the rules of number.

The activities will support you in developing your pupils' mathematical skills in understanding and using the properties of numbers. You will notice a particular focus on understanding multiplication and division facts and spotting and describing number patterns.

Each activity in the book is designed in the same way. On one page there is a task sheet you can use with your pupils. These are available to download from the companion website. On the facing page there is a prompt sheet for you. As in the previous chapter, this details:

- the target group for the task
- resources you will need
- possible starting points
- ways to represent the problem
- prompts to support you in developing mathematical thinking and reasoning
- prompts to support learners in communicating their learning
- prompts for recording: things to look for and encourage
- possible developments and alternative routes through the problem
- the mathematical skills that pupils will develop whilst engaged on the task.

As already suggested you should try these tasks out yourself or with colleagues so that you feel confident in the mathematics when you introduce them to your pupils. If you are reading or have read the companion volume *Understanding and Teaching Primary Mathematics* you may have already worked through many of these activities.

Be flexible – if the pupils discover things that you hadn't thought of don't be alarmed – be excited! Follow them on their new points of departure and enjoy learning mathematics together.

Task 5.1 Operations on a 100 square

Use the 100 square below for this activity. You will also need two dice and coloured crayons.

Roll the dice. Use the numbers on the dice to make two different two-digit numbers.

For example

I rolled a '3' and '6' so I can make 36 and 63.

1 Shade your starting number.
2 Add 10 to your starting number and colour the square in.
3 Subtract 11 from your starting number and colour the square in.
4 Add 21 to your starting number and colour the square in.
5 Subtract 19 from your starting number and colour the square in.
6 Use a new starting number and repeat using a different colour.

Repeat this for six different starting numbers.

1	2	3	4	5	6	7	8	9	10
11	12	13	14	15	16	17	18	19	20
21	22	23	24	25	26	27	28	29	30
31	32	33	34	35	36	37	38	39	40
41	42	43	44	45	46	47	48	49	50
51	52	53	54	55	56	57	58	59	60
61	62	63	64	65	66	67	68	69	70
71	72	73	74	75	76	77	78	79	80
81	82	83	84	85	86	87	88	89	90
91	92	93	94	95	96	97	98	99	100

Target group: Y1/2/Stages 1 and 2.

Resources: blank 100 squares, six-sided dice, crayons.

Possible starting point: use a large 100 square on the whiteboard and model the activity with the whole class. In this way you can introduce the language of rows and columns and moving up and down and forwards and backwards.

Represent the problem: encourage the pupils to use the 100 squares and to shade in the squares as they count.

Developing mathematical thinking and reasoning: ask pupils to move towards using the number square to support the calculation rather than counting on. They may want to count on or back at first and this should be encouraged. However work with the pupils to notice the patterns appearing on the 100 square. They can then generalise from the patterns that they notice to see that moving a column to the right adds one and moving one to the left subtracts one. Similarly, moving down one row adds 10 and moving up subtracts 10.

Communicating learning: ask the pupils to articulate their thinking. As they begin to generalise ask them to describe these generalisations to you. In a plenary session you can ask pupils to share these generalisations with each other.

Recording: as the pupils describe what they are noticing jot down their generalisations on the reverse of the 100 square or even in their mathematics notebook. At this stage you should be asking the pupils to describe what they are noticing and acting as a scribe for them.

Possible developments: ask pupils to think of their own addition or subtraction calculations and to describe how they can use the 100 square for their own calculations. Some pupils will also be able to generalise beyond 100.

Skills developed:

- counting and recognising numbers up to 100
- solving problems with addition and subtraction
- adding and subtracting numbers including a two-digit number and one and a two-digit number and ten
- finding 1 more/less and 10 more/less than any two-digit number.

Task 5.2 Square and triangular numbers

The first three square numbers are

S1 = 1   S2 = 4   S3 = 9

The first three triangle numbers are

T1 = 1   T2 = 3   T3 = 6 .

Draw and write down the first six square numbers.

Draw and write down the first six triangle numbers.

You can see that S3 = T2 + T3 (9 = 3 + 6)

Can you write down any square number as the sum of two square numbers?

Use a picture to illustrate your answer.

Target group: Y5/6/Stages 5 and 6.

Resources: scrap paper.

Possible starting point: as a whole class, work on drawing the first five square numbers and triangle numbers. Make sure that the pupils notice how the triangle numbers are formed (so T1 = 1; T2 = 2 + 1; T3 = 3 + 2 + 1 and so on). It may be worth pointing out that square numbers form a square. Not all pupils will have made this connection.

Represent the problem: it is really important that pupils use sketches to represent the problem. Seeing a square as two triangles joined together is useful when thinking about area too (this is why the area of a triangle is 1/2 base × height – it is half the area of a rectangle)

So this diagram shows that S5 = T4 + T5

Developing mathematical thinking and reasoning: ask the pupils to share their thinking with you. By articulating their thinking they will be able to move towards proof. Encourage the pupils to use terminology such as S2 and S3 and T2 and T3. You can do this through modelling. If a pupils says the fifth triangle number you can say – 'T5'.

Communicating learning: encourage pupils to share the diagrams that they are using. Ask them to use the language of proof. They should try to convince the other pupils in the group that this will always happen. Ask them why it would be true for all square numbers.

Recording: use the diagram above as a model for their recording. They should record informally at first whilst they are exploring the patterns. It would be helpful for them to use these jottings to make a formal report which describes their findings. This activity is useful for creating a wall display too.

Possible developments: ask the pupils for a generalisation. Can they work out which two triangle numbers you need to add together to find any square number?

Skills developed:

- recognising and using square numbers
- using logical reasoning to explore number problems
- identifying relationships between numbers and making generalised statements using words
- making, testing and refining hypotheses.

Task 5.3 The distributive law

You need a set of 1–9 digit cards for this activity.

This array shows that

$$13 \times 8 = (10 \times 8) + (3 \times 8) = 80 + 24 = 104$$

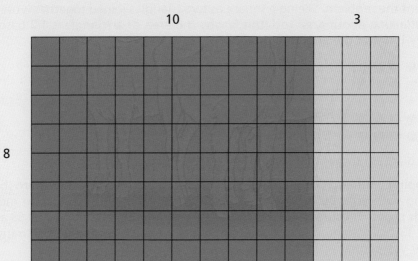

Pick any three digit cards. Use these digits to make six different multiplication calculations. Use the distributive law to calculate the answers.

For example: I picked **3**, **6** and **9**.

I can make

$$3 \times 69; \ 3 \times 96; \ 6 \times 39; \ 6 \times 93; \ 9 \times 63; \ 9 \times 36$$

Write down your three numbers:

Record your set of calculations:

Target group: Y3/4/Stages 3 and 4.

Resources: a set of digit cards for each pair. It is helpful to work in pairs or small groups on this activity as peers can check each other's answers and support each other.

Possible starting point: use the diagram on the stimulus sheet to explain the distributive property to the whole group. Model one or two more calculations using arrays such as this.

Represent the problem: if pupils find it difficult to visualise the distributive law encourage them to sketch arrays so that they can see how the multiplication is broken down. Working with the same digits in the calculation helps them see the way that the distributive law applies.

Developing mathematical thinking and reasoning: ask the pupils to explain why they can break the numbers down in the way that they do. Try to avoid them simply 'following a rule'. It is important that they see why the law applies and that it does not apply for all operations.

Communicating learning: ask pupils to carry out each other's calculations to check the answers. They should talk through each step so that their peers can hear them articulating their thinking.

Recording: ask pupils to be systematic in their recording. This form of calculation benefits from a systematic approach as it is then easier to see how you would break down any calculation of this form. This allows pupils to be able to use this strategy to calculate the multiplication of a two-digit number by a single-digit number.

Possible developments: ask the pupils to generalise. If you are given three consecutive single digits how would you arrange them to give you the largest possible product? They can also explore the differences between the answers. This should mean that they could arrange the calculations in ascending order according to their products without carrying out the calculation.

Skills developed:

- multiplying two-digit numbers by single-digit numbers mentally; moving on to written methods
- practising using and recalling multiplication facts
- choosing appropriate mental strategies to carry out calculations.

Task 5.4 Sorting numbers

Sort the numbers 2, 7, 8, 9, 17, 20 into this Carroll diagram

	Even	Not even
Prime		
Not prime		

Use examples to show whether these statements are true or false.

1   All prime numbers are odd.
2   All prime numbers are multiples of 3.
3   No multiples of 3 are even.

Write down your own definitions.

A prime number is ....

An even number is ....

An odd number is ....

Use Venn diagrams or Carroll diagrams to sort numbers in the following ways:

● multiples of 10 and multiples of 3

● multiples of 5 and multiples of 4

● odd numbers and multiples of 7.

Target group: Y3/4/Stages 3 and 4.

Resources: scrap paper (it is sometimes helpful to jot down the numbers on separate pieces of paper so that they can be moved around sections of the diagrams).

Possible starting point: use a large version of the Carroll diagram drawn on the whiteboard at the front of the class. Have a range of numbers that can be moved around the board and 'stuck' in the appropriate section. Repeat this with a Venn diagram so that the students are reminded of the difference between Carroll diagrams and Venn diagrams. Ask pupils what the advantages and disadvantages of each method are. This is a good activity for 'talk partners' or 'discussion pairs'.

Represent the problem: pupils will need to draft before using their jottings to create a more formal report. It may be appropriate for them to use mini whiteboards for drafting before committing the 'correct' diagram into the notebooks. In terms of representation one of the keys in this activity is noticing the different forms of classification the two diagrams offer. (Remember that Carroll diagrams should always be labelled 'criteria' and 'not criteria'.)

	Multiple of 10	Not multiple of 10
Multiple of 3		
Not multiple of 3		

Developing mathematical thinking and reasoning: the statements asking the pupils to use examples to prove or disprove the truth of the statements should be continued into the other classification activities. Ask pupils to make general statements (such as all multiples of 10 'end' in a zero) and look out for anything they notice that surprises them.

Communicating learning: at the end of the session pupils can be encouraged to share their general statements and anything that surprised them. They should offer these as questions similar to the stimulus page. Other pupils can try to explain why the statements might be true or false.

Recording: this activity can be more formally recorded by asking the pupils to come up with a stimulus sheet similar to the one that they have already used, based on their responses to the questions at the bottom of the stimulus page.

Possible developments: ask pupils to explore other number facts and number properties such as square numbers, triangle numbers, all the different multiples. They can choose the criteria for themselves and explore the relationships between the different criteria.

Skills developed:

- recalling multiplication and division facts
- recognising odd and even numbers
- using ordered lists and tables to help solve problems systematically
- investigating a simple general statement by finding examples which do not satisfy it.

Task 5.5 Patterns in multiplication facts

This is an activity for your whole class. You are going to explore all the patterns that you can find in multiples of all the numbers from 2 to 12. At the end of the session you should be able to write down at least two facts about each of the sets of multiples.

Multiples of 2:

Multiples of 3:

Multiples of 4:

Multiples of 5:

Multiples of 6:

Multiples of 7:

Multiples of 8:

Multiples of 9:

Multiples of 10:

Multiples of 11:

Multiples of 12:

Target group: Y3/4/Stages 3 and 4.

Resources: none needed. Perhaps a table square to support the groups who do not yet have good recall of all the multiplication facts.

Possible starting point: a great starting point (or endpoint) is the YouTube video www.youtube.com/watch?v=yXdHGBfoqfw You will have seen this if you have read the companion volume and the video is available on the companion website. This uses the counting stick to model the multiples of 17 and supports learners in using facts that they know to work out things they don't know.
Split the class up into small groups and give each group responsibility for a different set of multiples. It may be appropriate to work on this in two parts. Firstly multiples of 2 to 6 and then on the rest of the multiples to 12.

Represent the problem: pupils may want to use 100 squares to explore the patterns that exist in the family of multiples that they are looking at. They should also look at digit sums. (For example any number that is a multiple of 3 also has a digit sum that is a multiple of 3, e.g. 129 has a digit sum of $1 + 2 + 9 = 12$ which is a multiple of 3. This means that 129 is a multiple of 3.)

Developing mathematical thinking and reasoning: this comes through noticing and in particular describing the patterns that they are noticing and being able to translate what they notice into statements that they can share with each other. Encourage groups to articulate their thinking to you before they share it with the whole group.

Communicating learning: the activity should conclude by each group sharing what they have found with the whole class using examples to explain the facts they are describing. This means that the whole class can then have a full set of statements about the multiples of all numbers from 2 to 12.

Recording: again pupils will want to draft before they come up with their final statements which should be supported by examples.

Possible developments: pupils could explore multiples of 13, 15 and 17 which offer interesting patterns.

Skills developed:

- recalling multiplication and division facts
- recognising odd and even numbers
- using ordered lists and tables to help solve problems systematically
- investigating a simple general statement by finding examples which do not satisfy it.

Task 5.6 Partitioning

You need a full set of place value cards for this activity. You need a set that includes 'ones', 'tens', 'hundreds', and 'thousands'.

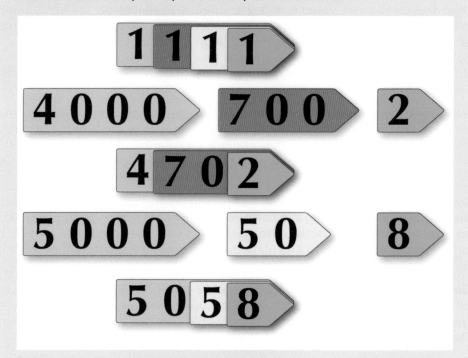

Tell the class: 'I made 5058 which is 5000 + zero hundreds + 5 tens + 8 ones. You say five thousand and fifty-eight.'

Pick a card from the thousands set and two each from the hundreds, tens and ones. List all the different numbers that you can make with these cards and write them in ascending order of size. Say the numbers aloud to your friends.

Pick one of the numbers to write down partitioned in thousands, hundreds, tens and ones and write down the number in words next to it. Draw an empty number line with the two thousands that your number lies between.

Target group: Y3/4/Stages 3 and 4.

Resources: sets of place value cards; full sets including ones, tens, hundreds and thousands. One set of cards for a small group.

Possible starting point: ask pupils to come to the front of the class and select one 'thousands' card, one 'hundreds', one 'tens' and one 'ones' card. Stick them to the whole board and then ask the students to say what the number would be. Write the number in digits and as a partition. Repeat this as many times as you think is necessary.

Represent the problem: ask the pupils to write some of the numbers they are making as partitions. This allows them to understand place value in four-digit numbers. They could also use empty number lines to represent the numbers.

Developing mathematical thinking and reasoning: this activity helps pupils think about how place value effects the 'size' of a number. You can help the pupils do this by asking them to take the numbers apart into the constituent parts and to put them back together. Make sure that all the pupils explore what happens when they have a zero as a place holder in either the tens or the hundreds column. If they do not select these numbers ask them the question so that they see the effect of zero hundreds. These are often the numbers that pupils struggle with.

Communicating learning: the activity should be carried out in small groups so that the pupils are saying the numbers aloud to each other. As you move around the groups make sure that you encourage the pupils to say the number aloud. In this way they get to 'hear' the place value of the numbers. This is particularly important for numbers such as

> **7089** or **7809**

Recording: encourage the students to record the numbers as partitions as well as writing the numbers down in words.

> **7809 = 7000 + 800 + 9 = 7809**

You say: seven thousand eight hundred and nine.

You may need to act as a scribe for some learners to encourage them to say the numbers aloud.

Possible developments: some pupils may be able to work with ten thousands in the same way. They can also explore rounding to the nearest thousand, hundred or ten by using empty number lines.

Skills developed:

- reading and writing numbers up to 10 000
- ordering and comparing numbers beyond 1000
- recognising the place value of each digit in a four-digit number
- rounding any number to the nearest 10, 100 or 1000
- estimating where three- and four-digit numbers lie on empty number lines.

Task 5.7 Totals 10 totals 100

Look at this board below.

1	2	4	3	4	5
5	6	1	7	8	6
8	5	4	3	9	4
2	7	3	9	1	8

Use coloured crayons.

- Colour in red four pairs of numbers that total 10.
- Colour in blue three numbers that total 10.
- Colour in green four numbers that total 10.

Make a board for your friend. This board should use numbers that can make totals to 100. Only use multiples of 10. These are 10, 20, 30, 40, 50, 60, 70, 80 and 90.

Target group: Y1/2/Stages 1 and 2.

Resources: the stimulus sheet and squared paper; crayons.

Possible starting point: create a large grid on the whiteboard. You could do this by randomly picking digit cards. You probably only need to draw a 4 by 4 board for the introduction. Ask pupils to come to the front and find pairs and triples that total 10. It may be appropriate to reintroduce the activity part way through the lesson when pupils move on to finding pairs to 100.

Represent the problem: pupils can use number lines and number tracks to find totals to 10. They may find 100 squares helpful to find totals to 100.

Developing mathematical thinking and reasoning: the important thing here is that pupils notice that if they know their totals to 10 then they can find totals to 100 simply by multiplying by 10. Convince them that this is true by using a 100 square. It is important that pupils come to this understanding themselves and know why this works. If they just remember it as a rule this may lead to misconceptions later.

Communicating learning: when pupils design their own boards for making totals to 100 they should think about the numbers that they are entering in the empty cells. They should work with each other when they complete these boards and give each other feedback on how effective their boards are. They can make improvements to these boards based on peer feedback.

Recording: pupils should make 'neat' copies of their final boards to take home and use with family or friends. This will encourage them to make changes based on feedback.

Possible developments: some pupils will be able to add in decimals to make totals to 1. Others could work with 'halves' or 'fifties' on the boards to total 10 and 100. Similarly, this activity can be developed to total 1000.

Skills developed:

- recalling and using addition facts to 20 and 100
- showing that addition can be carried out in any order
- finding all pairs of multiples of 10 that total 100.

Task 5.8 Boxes for stock cubes

You work for a company that produces and sells stock cubes.

They sell them in boxes of 24. The stock cubes are cubes of side 2cm.

Explore the different ways that you could package 24 stock cubes and produce a report which recommends the size of box that you would sell the stock cubes in.

You should take the surface area of the packaging into account.

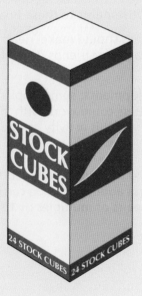

Target group: Y5/6/Stages 5 and 6.

Resources: interlocking cubes. Examples of packets of stock cubes – different sizes if you can find them.

Possible starting point: give groups of pupils 36 interlocking cubes and ask them to find as many different ways as they can of arranging these cubes as cuboids. Remind them that $1 \times 1 \times 36$ is possible. Talk about cuboids in different orientations. So $2 \times 2 \times 9$ would be the same cuboid whether it is upright or on its side. When pupils have explored this ask them to focus on the stock cube challenge. They may need reminding about how to calculate surface area and you could open up empty stock cube boxes to remind them of nets.

Represent the problem: pupils will need to come up with a way of recording all the different possible arrangements that they find. It may be appropriate to give them isometric paper to help them sketch the boxes. They will also need to draw the nets of the packages to explore the surface area.

Developing mathematical thinking and reasoning: the introductory activity supports the pupils in finding all the different arrangements. This makes a useful link to factors and multiples. It also helps pupils see the connection between dimension of cuboids and the volume. Ask pupils to describe their thinking as they work on the activity.

Communicating learning: each group should make a presentation at the end of the session to share their recommendations with the whole class. The class could vote at the end and decide which group's recommendation they will follow. This will encourage pupils to prepare a good presentation.

Recording: groups should prepare a formal presentation to the class. This could be a PowerPoint presentation. This will allow them to move from draft recording to more formal recording.

Possible developments: pupils could explore other forms of packaging. A trip to the supermarket or a local packaging company can provide opportunities to set this in a real-life context.

Skills developed:

- identifying common factors and common multiples
- recognising that shapes with the same area can have different perimeters and vice versa
- calculating volumes of cubes and cuboids
- recognising and building simple 3D shapes including making nets.

CHAPTER 6

NUMBER Calculating (addition, subtraction, multiplication, division)

These activities develop some of the tasks and resource ideas in *Understanding and Teaching Primary Mathematics,* the companion volume to this book. The activities in this chapter particularly focus on the development of pupils' mental and written methods for calculation.

The activities in this chapter will support you in developing your pupils' mathematical skills in calculating. The tasks support pupils to develop mental methods as a first resort and then have a bank of effective and efficient written methods that they can rely on when they need to follow a more formal written method.

As in previous chapters each activity is designed in the same way. On one page there is a task sheet you can use with your pupils. These are available to download from the companion website. On the facing page there is a prompt sheet for you. As in the previous chapter this details:

- the target group for the task
- resources you will need
- possible starting points
- ways to represent the problem
- prompts to support you in developing mathematical thinking and reasoning
- prompts to support learners in communicating their learning
- prompts for recording: things to look for and encourage
- possible developments and alternative routes through the problem
- the mathematical skills that pupils will develop whilst engaged on the task.

Make sure that you try out these tasks yourself or with colleagues so that you feel confident in the mathematics when you introduce them to your pupils. If you are reading or have read *Understanding and Teaching Primary Mathematics* you may have already worked through many of these activities.

Be flexible – if the pupils discover things that you hadn't thought of don't be alarmed – be excited! Follow them on their new points of departure and enjoy learning mathematics together.

Task 6.1 Mental methods

Work out the answers to the following calculations in your head. Don't write anything down.

11 + 6 =
28 − 9 =
20 × 5 =
57 × 3 =

Now talk to a partner. Tell them how you worked out the answer.

Did you do the same thing or did you use different strategies?

Now try these calculations.

For each calculation work it out yourself.

246 + 9 =
654 + 11 =
738 + 72 =
345 − 201 =
538 − 398 =
827 − 35 =
62 × 4 =
26 × 8 =
339 ÷ 3 =
750 ÷ 25 =

Check the answer with a partner and then discuss the strategies that you used.

Target group: Y3/4.

Resources: none – just the task sheet.

Possible starting point: you could share the first example and ask the whole class to calculate it mentally then discuss their strategies in pairs. Then share all the difference strategies. This models the learning process. It is possible to work on this activity as whole group exploring each calculation in turn. You may feel that it is appropriate to decide on pairs or threes before the activity and make groups that have a range of prior experiences.

Represent the problem: encourage pupils to draw number lines to explain the strategies that they used. This may help them explain. For example for

$$62 \times 4 = 248$$

they might draw

$$60 \qquad 8$$

This is something that you can model for the pupils on the whiteboard.

Developing mathematical thinking and reasoning: the discussion in pairs is vital to support the development of mathematical reasoning. If pupils can explain the strategies that they are using clearly they will be able to repeat those strategies when they see a similar calculation. The point here is that they are selecting effective strategies for a particular calculation rather than applying the same strategy to every calculation.

Communicating learning: pupils should discuss which strategy they think is most effective for each of the calculations. In a plenary session you should discuss which strategies you think are most effective for each of the calculations and 'name' the strategies.

Recording: try to record the strategies using number lines and display these around the room. Pupils can then refer to these to support them in future mental calculation activities.

Possible developments: ask pupils to set each other similar problems which draw on the strategies that they are using.

Skills developed:

- adding and subtracting numbers mentally including a three-digit number and ones; a three-digit number and tens
- recalling and using multiplication and division facts
- using place value and known and derived facts to multiply and divide mentally
- adding pairs of two-digit numbers using an appropriate strategy
- subtracting pairs of two-digit numbers using an appropriate strategy
- subtracting small numbers crossing 100.

Task 6.2 Making 20

You need 3 cups and 20 cubes for this activity.

Play with a partner. You can either pick up 1, 2 or 3 cubes.

Make your choice and put the cubes into one of the cups.

You win if there are no cubes left after your pick.

When you finish a game count the cubes in the cup and write down an addition sentence. For example

$$7 + 8 + 5 = 20.$$

Play the game five times.

Target group: Y1/2.

Resources: enough cups and cubes for each group.

Possible starting point: you could play a game against one of the class with the rest of the class watching to model the process. You may want to arrange the class into groups of four so that a pair are playing and a pair are observing at any one time. Having a pair observing helps the pupils to see a strategy.

Represent the problem: ask the pupils to try to work out a strategy to win the game each time. They could represent this using tallies or drawing circles around groups of 1, 2 or 3 cubes to represent the possible choices.

Developing mathematical thinking and reasoning: the pupils will begin to notice patterns to make 20. This will help them devise a strategy. For example if there are eight cubes left they will know that there are 12 in the cups. You can encourage this by asking them how many cubes have been used already at different times in the game. Encourage the pupils to think through a strategy each time rather than just picking random numbers of cubes.

Communicating learning: in a plenary session pupils can be encouraged to share strategies. You can also list all the pairs of numbers that add to 20 that they can remember. This activity should help them memorise these pairs. This is a useful fact to have available.

Recording: pupils can move from an iconic representation of the cubes in the cups to a more formal recording if necessary. Allow pupils to record in a range of ways so that you can show the progression from pictorial representation through iconic representation to the more formal number sentence.

Possible developments: this game can be played with larger numbers – or smaller numbers. For some pupils it may be appropriate to play with 2 cups and 10 cubes and for others 3 cups and 30 cubes.

Skills developed:

- recalling and using addition and subtraction facts to 20 fluently
- recognising and using the inverse relationship between addition and subtraction
- partitioning all numbers to 20 into pairs and recording the related facts.

Task 6.3 New facts for old

Work out each of these calculations in your head (mentally).

Talk to a partner to check your answer.

Then tell each other the strategy you used to work out the answer.

36 × 9
52 × 6
84 × 3

When you have checked the answer and described your strategy, take it in turns to derive new facts from the calculation.

For example if I know

27 × 9 = 243 (I multiplied 27 × 10 and subtracted 27)

I also know that

270 × 9 = 2430 (multiplying by 10)
27 × 18 = 486 (doubling the 9)
27 × 0.9 = 24.3 (dividing by 10)

Target group: Y3/4/Stages 3 and 4.

Resources: none needed.

Possible starting point: you could use the first example (or the example given in the text) and ask the whole class to work on it in pairs to model the process. Ask the pupils to discuss their strategies in pairs before they share their strategies with the whole class. Discuss the different strategies they use, in particular using near multiples of 10, or near doubles and partitioning.

For example you could calculate

$27 \times 9 = 243$

Multiply 27×10 and subtract $27 = 243$

$27 \times 9 = 20 \times 9 + 7 \times 9 = 180 + 63 = 180 + 20 + 43 = 243$

Represent the problem: you could sketch an array for the first example to show why the partitioning is an effective way of carrying out the calculation mentally. Similarly, you could illustrate the addition using an empty number line.

Developing mathematical thinking and reasoning: the discussion in pairs is vital to support the development of mathematical reasoning. If a pupil can explain the strategy that they are using clearly they will be able to repeat this strategy when they see a similar calculation. The point here is that they are selecting effective strategies for a particular calculation rather than applying the same strategy to every calculation.

Communicating learning: pupils should discuss which strategy they think is most effective for each of the calculations. In a plenary session you should discuss which strategies you think are most effective for each of the calculations and 'name' the strategies. Mention 'near doubles', 'near multiples of 10' and 'partitioning'.

Recording: try to record the strategies and display these around the room. Pupils can then refer to these to support them in future mental calculation activities.

Possible developments: ask pupils to set each other similar problems which draw on the strategies that they have used during the activity.

Skills developed:

- recalling multiplication and division facts
- using place value, known and derived facts to multiply and divide mentally
- finding the effect of dividing a one- or two-digit number by 10
- using knowledge of commutativity to find an easier way to multiply.

Task 6.4 Checking calculations

1   Look at these calculations. Can you say whether the answer will be even or odd without working out the answer?

$$4861 + 3758 \qquad\qquad 7052 - 507$$

$$34 \times 57 \qquad\qquad 711 - 296$$

$$72 \times 28 \qquad\qquad 461 + 836$$

How could you tell?

Write some calculations of your own that will give an even answer.

Write some calculations of your own that will give an odd answer.

2   Which of these answers are incorrect? Use the rules that you described in question 1 to help you.

$$30 \times 91 = 2730 \qquad\qquad 9072 - 978 = 8272$$

$$76 + 128 = 205 \qquad\qquad 826 + 7095 = 7922$$

$$68 \times 47 = 3196 \qquad\qquad 97 - 38 = 62$$

3   Can you explain why the rules you discovered in question 1 always work?

Target group: Y5/6.

Resources: cubes are useful to help 'prove' the rules governing calculating with odd and even numbers.

Possible starting point: you need a large space for this activity. Ask pupils to write a single digit on a piece of paper. Ask them to move around the space randomly and then pair up with someone close to them so that:

1   The sum of their digits is even.
2   The sum of their digits is odd.
3   The difference between their digits is even.
4   The difference between their digits is odd.
5   The product of their digits is even.
6   The product of their digits is odd.

You should ask pupils to move around between each question so that they are pairing up with different people. You can extend this to groups of three.
   At the end of the activity you can ask for 'rules' that people are following.

Represent the problem: encourage pupils to work on the activity in small groups. They can check that their assumptions are correct using a calculator and jot down the 'rules' that they are using.

Developing mathematical thinking and reasoning: try to get the pupils to model any explanations of why the rules always work visually. They should realise that

- even + even = even
- even + odd = odd
- difference between even numbers is even
- difference between odd numbers is even
- even × even = even
- even × odd = even
- odd × odd = odd

They can model the addition and subtraction rules using cubes and building towers. Seeing 'evenness' as two towers of equal height is a beginning of a proof. Thinking about multiplication as repeated addition helps to describe the rules for multiplication and division.

Communicating learning and recording: this is the most important part of this activity as it asks pupils to think deeply about the mathematics and move towards proof. The pupils should try out their explanations in a small group before sharing their explanations with the whole class. They will also need to illustrate their thinking visually or using concrete materials.

Possible developments: the rules can be extended for three or four numbers by applying the rules to pairs of numbers in turn.

Skills developed:

- adding and subtracting numbers with increasingly large numbers
- multiplying and dividing numbers mentally
- checking answers to calculations
- knowing and applying arithmetical laws.

Task 6.5 Arrays and fact families

You will need a box of cubes for this activity. An array is made up of rows and columns.

These stamps are in a 3 × 8 array. I can use this array to write a fact family. So

3 × 8 = 24
8 × 3 = 24
24 ÷ 8 = 3
24 ÷ 3 = 8

How many different arrays can you make with 16 cubes?

What about 32?

Write down the fact families for each of the arrays.

Try other numbers of cubes.

Which numbers can you use to make lots of different arrays?

Which numbers don't give you very many arrays?

Target group: Y3/4/Stages 3 and 4.

Resources: cubes; about 40 for each group working on the activity.

Possible starting point: you can model the stamps array physically. Ask 24 of the pupils to come into a space and arrange themselves in different arrays. Sketch each array on the whiteboard and ask pupils to work in pairs to write down the different fact families.

Representing and recording the problem: the pupils should draw each of the arrays that they form with the cubes and write the fact families underneath. This helps them see the 'facts' as a mental image.

Developing mathematical thinking and reasoning: ask pupils to explore different numbers of cubes. They will begin to make the link between numbers of factors and the different arrays they can make. They will even make a start to seeing what a prime number is (a number which has only a single array).

Communicating learning: a plenary session is important for pupils to discuss and share what they have found out. As in previous activities encourage them to start sharing theory ideas in small groups so that they are more confident when it comes to describing their findings to the whole class.

Possible developments: this activity can be developed for cuboids. This is particularly useful for beginning to model volume. Similarly, the links between the arrays and area and perimeter can be made. The arrays are also helpful for exploring fractions.

Skills developed:

- recalling multiplication and division facts to 12×12
- recognising and using factor pairs.

Task 6.6 Largest product

What is the largest product that can be made using the digits

    3 4 5 6

You can multiply 2 two-digit numbers together or a three-digit number by a single digit number.

For example 34 × 65 or 465 × 3

Does what you found out work for any four consecutive numbers?

Why do you think it works?

Target group: Y3/4.

Resources: none needed. I use calculators for this activity although you can ask pupils to use paper and pencil methods if you prefer.

Possible starting point: ask pupils in pairs to think of as many different multiplication calculations as they can using the consecutive digits. Ask pupils to estimate which they think will give the larger products and give a reason why.

Represent the problem: this depends on whether you are using calculators or not. The focus here is on place value so you may want to use place value grids to record the answers to emphasise this point.

Developing mathematical thinking and reasoning: encouraging pupils to notice the difference between what they are expecting and what they notice after carrying out the calculation allows them to see how place value impacts on multiplication. You can support this by asking pupils to estimate an answer before they carry out a calculation.

Communicating learning: at the end of the activity pupils should try to summarise their discoveries and explore whether or not these discoveries work for all sets of consecutive numbers.

Recording: it may be helpful to arrange the calculations in order of size of product so that the pupils can see the 'differences' between the answers and see how place value impacts on multiplication. Carrying out the calculations using the column method or the grid method will illustrate where the 'difference' can be found.

Possible developments: beginning to generalise by using other sets of consecutive numbers or even non-consecutive numbers is a great development.

Skills developed:

- recalling multiplication and division facts up to 12×12
- using place value to multiple mentally
- multiplying two-digit by two-digit and one-digit by three-digit numbers
- choosing appropriate strategies to multiply numbers.

Task 6.7 How many chickpeas fill the classroom?

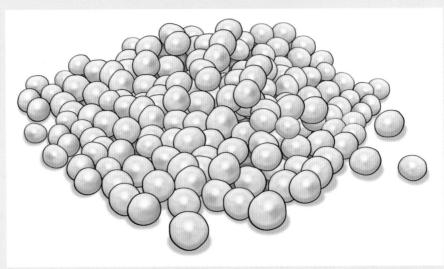

How many chickpeas do you think it would take to fill your classroom?

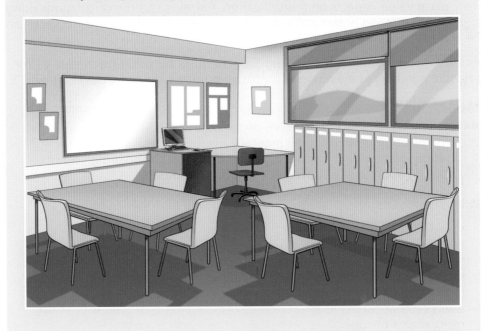

Target group: Y5/6.

Resources: packets of chickpeas. One pack per group would be great. Also sets of containers so that groups can begin to estimate how many would fill one cubic metre.

Possible starting point: this is best tackled with an open starting point. Simply pose the question to the groups and get them to think about it in groups before you give the pupils any ideas. Avoid the temptation to give them ways to get started.

Represent the problem: once the pupils have realised that they need to start to think about how many chickpeas will fill a smaller container and then work up to cubic metres and then find the volume of the classroom, encourage them to make 3D sketches of the classroom.

Developing mathematical thinking and reasoning: if you leave this open at the beginning of the activity pupils will begin to reason mathematically in order to arrive at a way of solving the problem. They will also begin to get a sense of the amount of volume something takes up – as well as beginning to get a sense of large numbers.

Communicating learning: this is a great activity to ask groups to share solutions at the end of the exercise. Give groups time to prepare their presentations to the rest of the class. At the end of all the presentations the class can decide on the most appropriate estimation for the number of chickpeas that will fit in the classroom.

Recording: groups should draw on the sketches and jottings that they have used in solving the problem to prepare 'neat copy' that can be used for wall displays and to share with parents and other adults.

Possible developments: this leads onto exploration of big numbers. You could ask questions like:

- Where could I get to if I was to walk a million paces?
- Can I live to be a million days old?
- How many breaths might I take in a year?

Skills developed:

- solving problems involving calculation and conversion of units of measure
- estimating volumes of cuboids
- solving problems which require answers to be rounded
- solving problems involving addition, subtraction, division and multiplication
- using estimation to check answers to calculations and determine in the context of a problem an appropriate degree of accuracy.

Task 6.8 Best value purchase

Lowest Price
Pile of Keys
×50
£1.49

14% More!
Suitcase of Keys
×285
£6.99

12% More!
Box of Keys
×140
£2.99

Look at the offer above. Decide which offer you would choose if you had to buy keys for

100 people

150 people

200 people

250 people

500 people

If you were charging people for the keys, how much would you charge each person?

Explore other special offers from supermarkets.

Target group: Y5/6/Stages 5 and 6.

Resources: selection of adverts or photographs from supermarkets showing special offers and bulk buys. Pupils will need calculators for this activity.

Possible starting point: start as a whole class exploring the problem. You may ask different groups to look at each of the questions and then report back to the whole class about what they have found. If you have managed to find a range of other special offers ask different groups to work on different offers so that they can share a range of solutions at the end of the activity.

Represent the problem: this is mainly a calculation problem which requires pupils to work out a unit cost so there may not be much requirement to represent the problem pictorially.

Developing mathematical thinking and reasoning: allow pupils to explore the problem in small groups for themselves. They may come up with different solutions to take into account wastage. Make sure that you allow different solutions to emerge and discuss the advantages and disadvantages of the solutions.

Communicating learning: each group should report back at the end of the activity. As this activity explores a real-life context the communication can be related to their everyday experience.

Recording: you can ask groups to create best value posters to share with each other.

Possible developments: you could use this activity to set up a class healthy tuck shop and use these kinds of budgeting skills in a real context.

Skills developed:

- solving problems involving calculation and conversion of units of measure
- solving problems using decimal notation
- solving multi-step problems in a real context
- solving problems which require answers to be rounded
- solving problems involving addition, subtraction, division and multiplication
- using estimation to check answers to calculations and determine in the context of a problem an appropriate degree of accuracy.

Task 6.9 Additions

Choose four of these numbers.

1 3 4 6 7 9

How many different totals can you make?

You could add together four single-digit numbers

1 + 3 + 7 + 9 = 20

or a mixture of one-digit and two-digit numbers

13 + 46 + 7 = 66

Target group: Y1/2.

Resources: some pupils may find concrete objects helpful to support their calculations. You should have number lines and 100 squares available to support the calculations too.

Possible starting point: you could start as a whole class and ask pairs to make as many different totals as they can in five minutes to model the process.

Represent the problem: some pupils may want to show the calculations using number lines or by illustrating the addition using a 100 square.

Developing mathematical thinking and reasoning: encourage pupils to work systematically to explore how many different totals that can get. For example they could focus on single-digit additions and look at how many possibilities there are for choosing four numbers from six. Others may look at different arrangements of two-digit numbers and so on. Ask the pupils to tell you how they know that they have found all the possibilities.

Communicating learning: a plenary session should include pupils sharing their answers as well as the justification for having found all the different possibilities. This means that they have to share how they have organised their work systematically.

Recording: ask pupils to use their jottings to create a 'neat' copy of their solution to the problem that can be shared more widely or that can be used for a wall display.

Possible developments: similar activities could be used involving subtraction, or multiplication or a mixture of arithmetical operations.

Skills developed:

- recalling and using addition facts to 20 fluently
- adding a two-digit number and ones, two two-digit numbers and three one-digit numbers
- adding four small numbers together
- understanding that addition can be carried out in any order.

CHAPTER 7
ALGEBRA

As with the previous chapters the activities in this chapter develop some of the tasks and resource ideas from Chapter 6 in *Understanding and Teaching Primary Mathematics,* which helped you understand how to develop your own algebraic thinking. The activities here should help you explore algebraic thinking with the pupils that you are working with. There is a particular focus on specialising and generalising.

Each activity is designed in the same way as all the activities in the book. On one page there is a 'task sheet' you can use with your pupils. These are available to download from the companion website. On the facing page there is a prompt sheet for you. As in the previous chapters this details:

- the target group for the task
- resources you will need
- possible starting points
- ways to represent the problem
- prompts to support you in developing mathematical thinking and reasoning
- prompts to support learners in communicating their learning
- prompts for recording: things to look for and encourage
- possible developments and alternative routes through the problem
- the mathematical skills that pupils will develop whilst engaged on the task.

Make sure that you try out these tasks yourself or with colleagues so that you feel confident in the mathematics when you introduce the activities to your pupils. If you are reading or have read the companion volume *Understanding and Teaching Primary Mathematics* you may have already worked through many of these activities.

Try to be flexible – if the pupils discover things that you hadn't thought of don't be alarmed – be excited! Follow them on their new points of departure and enjoy learning mathematics together.

Task 7.1 Patterns in a 100 square

Look at this 100 square.

1	2	3	4	5	6	7	8	9	10
11	12	13	14	15	16	17	18	19	20
21	22	23	24	25	26	27	28	29	30
31	32	33	34	35	36	37	38	39	40
41	42	43	44	45	46	47	48	49	50
51	52	53	54	55	56	57	58	59	60
61	62	63	64	65	66	67	68	69	70
71	72	73	74	75	76	77	78	79	80
81	82	83	84	85	86	87	88	89	90
91	92	93	94	95	96	97	98	99	100

Pick any line of three numbers.

43   44   45

Add the numbers together. What do you notice about the total?

If you know the middle number can you work out the total?

Why does this rule work?

Try lines of four numbers and five and six.

What do you notice about your answers?

Why do you think this happens?

Target group: Year 5/6/Stages 5 and 6.

Resources: calculators, squared paper and 100 squares.

Possible starting point: ask pupils to work in pairs. Give them all a 100 square and a calculator. I use calculators for this activity as I am interested in developing algebraic thinking rather than practising mental methods. (Of course, the activity does offer a useful mental method for adding consecutive numbers.) Ask pupils to work on this in pairs for 10 minutes or so. They should try two or three different sets of consecutive numbers. This means that when the pairs report back there will be several different sets that have been explored. In the report back focus on why the total should be three times the middle number. Try not to feed the answer but allow plenty of thinking time. You may want to introduce

$$n - 1 \qquad\qquad n \qquad\qquad n + 1$$

but do allow pupils to use their own language for the generalisation.

Represent the problem: use 100 squares to locate the sets of consecutive numbers and encourage learners to copy out the 'chunks' that they are exploring. I think this makes it easier to see the patterns in the consecutive numbers. It may be useful to rewrite some of the numbers as, for example,

$$47 - 1 \qquad\qquad 47 \qquad\qquad 47 + 1$$

Developing mathematical thinking and reasoning: you will need to encourage the pupils to explain their thought processes and to move towards generalisation. Often pupils are happy to notice the pattern (it's three times the middle number) and less eager to explain why this is the case. Explaining why is at the heart of mathematics so be persistent!

Communicating learning: this will be very tentative at this stage. Encourage the pupils to try to convince each other of the reasons that the rules they are discovering always work. Why are their generalisations true?

Recording: I think the main focus of communication for this activity should be verbal communication as the pupils begin to convince each other of the patterns and rules that they have found. It may be appropriate to try to agree as a whole class how you can record this in a written form. This is a good way of refining the language that the pupils will be using.

Possible developments: pupils could explore other shapes in the square such as

Skills developed:

- using simple formulae
- generating and describing number sequences
- deducing new information from existing information and realising the effect one piece of information has on another
- identifying relationships between numbers and making generalised statements using words, symbols and letters
- making, testing and refining hypotheses.

Task 7.2 Growing shapes

Look at this series of shapes.

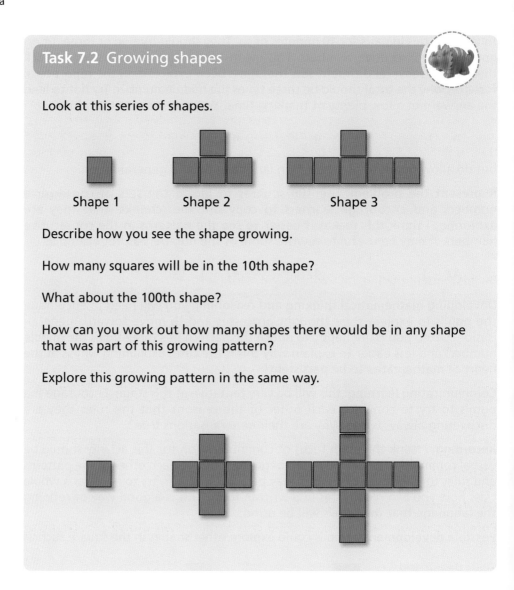

Shape 1   Shape 2   Shape 3

Describe how you see the shape growing.

How many squares will be in the 10th shape?

What about the 100th shape?

How can you work out how many shapes there would be in any shape that was part of this growing pattern?

Explore this growing pattern in the same way.

Target group: Y5/6/Stages 5 and 6.

Resources: calculators. Squared paper and 100 squares would be useful.

Possible starting point: this is an activity which does not really need an introduction as you want each group to explore the growing patterns in their own way. I would simply set the groups off to explore this on their own with minimal input. At various stages during the session you may want to ask groups to share their thinking as a way of developing their communication and mathematical thinking.

Represent the problem: use squares or cubes to 'build' the patterns. The physical movement of the blocks helps pupils 'see' the way that the patterns are growing. Encourage pupils to record their thoughts 'verbatim' at first. You can help by writing down their explanations for them to allow them to focus on verbalising their thinking.

Developing mathematical thinking and reasoning: you will need to encourage the pupils to explain their thought processes and to move towards generalisation. As with the previous activity they may quickly spot a pattern and then move on. The most important thing about developing algebraic thinking is explaining why the generalisation is true.

Communicating learning: this will be very tentative at this stage. Encourage the pupils to try to convince each other of the reasons that the rules they are discovering always work. Why are their generalisations true? Allow them to use a range of explanations. They should not all move to using symbols or letters.

Recording: as with the previous activity the main focus of communication for this activity should be verbal communication as the pupils begin to convince each other of the patterns and rules that they have found. Avoid jumping to recording the results in tables as this may get in the way of pupils seeing the generalisation.

Possible developments: pupils could create their own growing patterns to explore and for each other to explore.

Skills developed:

- using simple formulae
- generating and describing number sequences
- deducing new information from existing information and realising the effect one piece of information has on another
- identifying relationships between numbers and making generalised statements using words, symbols and letters
- making, testing and refining hypotheses.

Task 7.3 How many ears?

I have four cats at home. I wonder how many ears they have?

How many ears would three cats have?

What about five?

Is there a pattern?

Each cat has six whiskers.

How many whiskers would my four cats have altogether?

Target group: Y1/2/Stages 1 and 2.

Resources: plain paper to draw cats; lots of pictures of cats; other pictures of animals or pictures that can be used in the same way.

Possible starting point: I would use this as part of a circus of activities rather than an activity that the whole class would work on at the same time. This should be a practical activity rather than an activity in which you give out a stimulus sheet. Much better to set it up using photographs of cats and asking the question yourself. Have a series of other photographs of animals that the pupils can use to set themselves questions.

Represent the problem: the best way to support the pupils in representing the problem is to use the images or to allow them to draw the cats. They may prefer to use a simplified version as in the stimulus page or even move towards iconic representation using 'disembodied' ears or just marks.

Developing mathematical thinking and reasoning: mathematical reasoning is developed as pupils notice that they are multiplying the number of cats by 2 – or counting up in twos. Pupils may need supporting to notice this pattern and to move away from just counting.

Communicating learning: it may be helpful for you to join in the game and make 'guesses'. 'I think there will be ten ears on five cats – how do you think I knew that?' This is a way of triggering young learners to communicate what they are thinking.

Recording: encourage the pupils to make as many jottings as they need. You may want to take photographs of these jottings to talk to the pupils about when they work on similar activities.

Possible developments: the pupils can use lots of different kinds of animals and start to pose their own questions.

Skills developed:

- using number facts to solve problems
- solving problems with addition
- recalling and using multiplication facts
- explaining methods and reasoning orally
- exploring number problems and puzzles
- making sense of simple word problems.

Task 7.4 Bead strings

Here is a pattern made from a bead string.

Can you:

- make this pattern
- make different patterns of your own
- explain how your pattern grows
- give your pattern to a friend – can they carry it on?

Target group: Y1/2/Stages 1 and 2.

Resources: pieces of string and lots of different coloured beads.

Possible starting point: as with the previous activity I would use this as part of a circus of activities rather than an activity that the whole class would work on at the same time. This should be a practical activity rather than an activity in which you give out a stimulus sheet. In fact this could be an activity that you would set up at the same time as the previous activity.

Representing and recording the problem: the best way to support the pupils in representing the problem is to take photographs of their bead strings and ask them to describe the patterns. You can then annotate the photographs.

Developing mathematical thinking and reasoning: mathematical reasoning is developed as pupils can describe their patterns to each other and predict how to continue a pattern that someone else is creating.

Communicating learning: it may be helpful for you to join in making bead strings and talk about how you are constructing a pattern to model the sort of language that you are hoping for. For example, 'I am going to use three red, and then three blue and then three green. Then I will start again with three red beads.'

Possible developments: the pupils can create patterns using shapes, making shapes in the sand, or even devise simple number patterns using cherries on cakes or something similar.

Skills developed:

- describing and making repeating patterns
- explaining what shape or colour should come next in a pattern.

Task 7.5 Balances

You need a pan balance for this activity.

Use different objects in the classroom. You could use cubes, or toy cars, or shapes, or any other small object.

Put two or three of the same object in one side of the balance. See how many of another object you need to balance this.

Draw a picture or write down what you find out.

Target group: Y1/2/Stages 1 and 2.

Resources: pan balances and a range of small objects: cubes, toy animals, small shapes, toy cars and so on.

Possible starting point: as with the previous activities this could be a part of a circus of activities rather than an activity that the whole class would work on at the same time. The focus must be practical and exploratory rather than an activity in which you give out the stimulus sheet. This and the previous activities could form part of a carousel themselves or could be offered over a number of weeks alongside other activities. This activity can be repeated on several occasions so that the pupils build on their previous experience.

Representing and recording the problem: the best way to support the pupils in representing the problem is to ask them to draw the balance scales and the items that balance. Some pupils may move on to working with jottings to record their result. This could be in the form of a picture.

Developing mathematical thinking and reasoning: mathematical reasoning is developed as pupils can describe what they are finding to each other and predict how many more objects they think they will need to balance. You can encourage this by careful questioning – asking 'How many more do you think you will need to balance?' 'Why do you think that will balance?' and so on.

Communicating learning: it may be helpful for you to join in the activity to model the mathematical vocabulary. 'I am going to put two cars on that side. I think that four cubes will balance,' and so on.

Possible developments: pupils could work with balance beams that give gradated scales to develop their thinking.

Skills developed:

- using everyday language to talk about a wide range of measures
- using properties of objects to solve problems and make comparisons.

Task 7.6 How far around your head?

What do you think the ratio of the circumference of your head to your height is?

This is very useful information for hat makers!

Work with some friends.

Measure the circumference of their heads.

Measure their heights.

Draw a scatter diagram to work out the ratio.

Do you think this ratio is always the same?

What about young children?

Will it be the same for women and men?

Target group: Y3/4/Stages 3 and 4.

Resources: measuring tapes and metre rules for measuring height; large pieces of squared paper for the scatter diagram.

Possible starting point: ask for estimates from the class before you start the investigation. This activity is best carried out as a whole class activity. Illustrate how to plot a point on the scatter diagram; perhaps by taking your own measurements and plotting them. You will also need to agree on the scales that you will use. Again you can use your own data to come up with sensible scales.

Representing and recording the problem: I have found it helpful to use initials against the plotted points so that each pupil can see their 'own' data. In this way the scatter diagram gradually builds an image of the data. I have also colour coded male and female results so that the pupils can see if there is any difference here. Similarly, they could measure a class very much lower down the school and see if there is any difference in the data, or collect the data from all the teachers in the school.

Developing mathematical thinking and reasoning: the thinking and reasoning comes from interpreting the data. Once all the data is collected and the scatter diagram has been constructed you can show how to draw a line of best fit and then how you use this to find the ratio. (You will find that it is about 3:1.)

Communicating learning: ask pupils to summarise their learning to each other. They should discuss what they have found out and why they think this finding is accurate. They can also discuss the sorts of questions that they can ask next and design ways to explore these questions.

Possible developments: you can explore the relationships between other measurements on the body. Or they could explore this question in more depth by looking at different groups of people.

Skills developed:

- solving scaling problems and using ratio and proportion in simple contexts
- beginning to generalise mathematical situations
- beginning to express relationships as a formula (height = 3 circumferences of head or $H = 3C$).

Task 7.7 Christmas crackers

Tony is wondering how many Christmas crackers to buy for his party.

He wants everyone at his party to pull a cracker with everyone else.

There will be 24 people at his party.

How many crackers do you think he should buy?

Can you find a way to work out the number of crackers you need for any number of people?

Target group: Y3/4/Stages 3 and 4.

Resources: lots of scrap paper for jottings; large sheets of paper to begin to record the results.

Possible starting point: this is another activity which needs little introduction. I always work with all attainment groups of four or five on this activity. You may want to remind pupils of how to work well in groups. They could pick a group leader whose job it is to make sure everyone has a say. Another member of the group could be the scribe and a third member could take responsibility for reporting back.

Allow the groups to work on their own at first. If they do not make any progress you could suggest that they start with the simplest case. How many crackers for one person, then two, then three and then for their small group. This may help them start to see a pattern.

Representing and recording the problem: children often write lists of their names and draw lines to connect them. A circle with 'nodes' to represent the others in the group is also a good way of representing the problem. If children choose this way of recording you can introduce them to the 'mystic rose'. There are lots of beautiful examples on the internet.

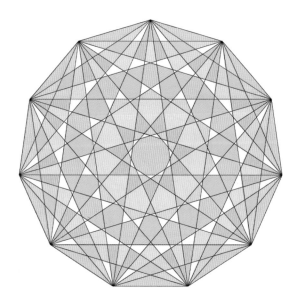

Developing mathematical thinking and reasoning: encourage pupils to articulate their thinking throughout the activity. Ask them to convince you about what they have found out and ask them for a rationale for their next step. Through articulating their thinking they develop their mathematical thinking and reasoning.

Communicating learning: as with the other activities the communication will primarily take place during the activity and can be prompted by your careful questioning. At the end of the session you should ask pupils to summarise their learning to each other. They should discuss what they have found out and why they think this finding is accurate. The focus on convincing others that their findings are accurate is the key part of communication here.

Possible developments: there are many similar problems such as the handshake problem or other investigations involving making choices. For example if there are two starters, three main courses and two desserts how many different meals could I choose?

Skills developed:

- beginning to generalise mathematical situations
- beginning to express relationships as a formula
- solving scaling problems and using ratio and proportion in simple contexts
- using simple formulae
- generating and describing number sequences.

Task 7.8 Goats and chickens

A farmer has only chickens and goats on her farm. She has 28 animals and there are 72 legs altogether.

How many chickens and goats are there?

Target group: Y3/4/Stages 3 and 4.

Resources: cubes are useful for modelling the animals, particularly ones that can be joined together. I sometimes use modelling clay and modelling sticks to create small animals.

Possible starting point: this is another activity which needs little introduction. I use all attainment groups and encourage groups to get started in any way that they think is sensible. Exploring the problem freely is a great way to begin to develop mathematical reasoning. If some groups cannot get started ask them to visit groups who are making progress so that this group can explain their current thinking.

Represent the problem: either use cubes or modelling clay to create animals so that you begin to count the legs. Pupils can then change chickens into goats by joining together '2 chickens'. In this way they see that 2 chickens = 1 goat!

Developing mathematical thinking and reasoning: it is very unlikely that the pupils will be able to see the answer immediately. This means that they have to begin to work systematically and to try different situations. Ask the pupils to articulate their thinking as they are working on the problem. This articulation in itself often helps pupils move forwards.

Communicating learning: as well as articulating their thinking to each other as they move through the process, ask pupils to try to reflect on their learning at the end of the session and to identify moments at which they moved forwards. John Mason has called these 'aha' moments. If we can spot these we are able to transfer our problem-solving methods to other situations. Similarly, noticing when we are stuck and how we became 'unstuck' is extremely helpful.

Recording: encourage pupils to keep jottings as they solve the task. Ask them to use these jottings to develop a more formal 'report' of how they came to a solution. This helps them both record the process and to 'notice' how they solved the problem.

Possible developments: there are many similar activities involving correspondence between two or three items. Even better, ask pupils to set each other similar problems.

Skills developed:

- using number facts to solve number problems
- solving scaling problems and using ratio and proportion in simple contexts
- working on correspondence problems
- generalising mathematical situations.

CHAPTER 8
GEOMETRY

The activities in this chapter develop some of the tasks and the resource ideas from Chapter 7 in *Understanding and Teaching Mathematics* which helped you develop your understanding of geometrical ideas. The activities here should help you explore geometry with the pupils that you are working with. There is a particular focus on the properties of 2D and 3D shapes, ideas of symmetry and position and movement.

Each activity is designed in the same way as all the activities in the book. On one page there is a task sheet you can use with your pupils. These are available to download from the companion website. On the facing page there is a prompt sheet for you. As in the previous chapter this details:

- the target group for the task
- resources you will need
- possible starting points
- ways to represent the problem
- prompts to support you in developing mathematical thinking and reasoning
- prompts to support learners in communicating their learning
- prompts for recording: things to look for and encourage
- possible developments and alternative routes through the problem
- the mathematical skills that pupils will develop whilst engaged on the task.

Make sure that you try out these tasks yourself or with colleagues so that you feel confident in the geometrical ideas yourself when you introduce the activities to your pupils. If you are reading or have read the companion volume *Understanding and Teaching Primary Mathematics* you will have already worked through many of these activities.

And be flexible – if the pupils discover things that you hadn't thought of don't be alarmed – be excited! Follow them on their new points of departure and enjoy learning mathematics together.

Task 8.1 Say what you see; draw what you see

You need to work in groups of four for this activity. Three of the group should close their eyes. The other member of the group reads the following:

Imagine a large red rectangle in your mind. Stand it on its end so that you can see it standing on its shortest side. Slowly rotate it so that it is resting on one of the longest sides. Rotate it again so that it is balancing on a corner. Continue to rotate the rectangle and decide when you want it to stop. Now imagine a small, blue, right-angled triangle that will fit inside the rectangle. Picture it inside the rectangle and slide it so that the right angle fits exactly into one of the corners of the rectangle. Picture another small, blue, right-angled triangle which is a different size from the first triangle. Slide it to fit into one of the other corners of the rectangle. Notice the red shape that is formed inside the rectangle.

Open your eyes and sketch the image that was in your head.

Talk about the different red shapes that you have made.

Take it in turns to invent different visualisations for the others in your group to carry out.

Target group: Y3/4/Stages 3 and 4.

Resources: mini whiteboards.

Possible starting point: you could choose to carry out the initial visualisation with the whole group. They could work in pairs to talk about the shapes that they make. This allows you to model the mathematical language with the whole group. The small groups could then work on their own visualisation activities.

Represent the problem: it is important to get the pupils to sketch what they are seeing. This allows them to explore each other's visualisations. It also allows all the pupils to have access to each other's shapes.

Developing mathematical thinking and reasoning and communicating learning: the discussion focusing on describing properties of shapes and noticing similarities and differences of the shapes by exploiting their properties is an important part of developing mathematical thinking. This activity also supports pupils in becoming skilled at visualising, which is an important mathematical technique. The activity also provides pupils with a reason to communicate their thinking which helps them to develop an appropriate mathematical vocabulary.

Recording: pupils should record a series of shapes that they made during the activity. They can note down the similarities and differences between the shapes. This also makes an excellent wall display.

Possible developments: how many different polygons could be made using this visualisation? Pupils could explore all the different polygons that they can make. They could also explore which polygons cannot be made. These questions can also be asked of the visualisations which they come up with.

Skills developed:

- comparing and classifying geometric shapes, including quadrilaterals and triangles, based on their properties and sizes
- identifying acute and obtuse angles and comparing and ordering angles up to two right angles by size
- identifying lines of symmetry in 2D shapes presented in different orientations
- identifying, describing, visualising, drawing and making a wider range of 2D and 3D shapes including a range of quadrilaterals, the heptagon and tetrahedron
- classifying polygons (including a range of quadrilaterals) using criteria such as the number of right angles, whether or not they are regular and their symmetrical properties.

Task 8.2 Classifying polygons

Look at these polygons.

Classify them in any way you like and in as many groups as you like.

Record your classification.

Talk to a friend about the criteria that you used to classify the shapes.

Name as many of the polygons as you can.

Target group: Y3/4/Stages 3 and 4.

Resources: it would be useful to make copies of the shapes on card so that pupils can cut the shapes up in order to classify them. (There is a photocopiable sheet on the companion website.)

Possible starting point: ask all the pupils to draw a polygon on a small piece of paper. They should fold this paper up and then move around the classroom. When you ask them to stop they should pair up and look at each other's polygons. They should name one property that their two polygons share and one property which they do not share. Repeat this so that you can model the key mathematical vocabulary that you will want the pupils to draw on during the classification activity.

Represent the problem: the pupils should decide on different ways to represent the classification that they use. They may use Venn diagrams, Carroll diagrams or some other sorting diagram. They will need to take care in labelling the diagram. Discourage the pupils from using a category such as 'miscellaneous'.

Developing mathematical thinking and reasoning and communicating learning: the discussion focusing on describing properties of shapes and noticing similarities and differences of the shapes by exploiting their properties is an important part of developing mathematical thinking. This activity also supports pupils in becoming skilled at visualising, which is an important mathematical technique. The activity also provides pupils with a reason to communicate their thinking which supports them in developing an appropriate mathematical vocabulary.

Recording: this is another activity which lends itself to creating wall displays. Each group can choose one of the ways of classifying the shapes and create a wall poster which incorporates the names of all the polygons.

Possible developments: the pupils could create a similar activity for 3D shapes. When creating activities it is always important to create a draft activity and trial this with a small group. They can then take feedback as to how the activity can be improved before creating a final version.

Skills developed:

- comparing and classifying geometric shapes, including quadrilaterals and triangles, based on their properties and sizes
- identifying acute and obtuse angles and comparing and ordering angles up to two right angles by size
- identifying lines of symmetry in 2D shapes presented in different orientations
- identifying, describing, visualising, drawing and making a wider range of 2D and 3D shapes including a range of quadrilaterals, the heptagon and tetrahedron
- classifying polygons (including a range of quadrilaterals) using criteria such as the number of right angles, whether or not they are regular and their symmetrical properties.

Task 8.3 Sorting triangles

This activity is for groups of four or five. Each member of the group should draw four different triangles on four postcards.

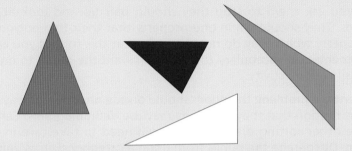

When you have all drawn the triangles take it in turns to sort the triangles into groups. The others in your group should guess the criteria you are using to sort the triangles.

Can you name all the different types of triangles?

Are there any triangles that you didn't draw?

Pick two different triangles.

Write down three facts about each triangle.

Target group: Y1/2/Stages 1 and 2.

Resources: mini whiteboards, blank postcards or small pieces of scrap paper.

Possible starting point: ask each pupil to draw a triangle on their mini whiteboard. They should then turn to a partner and find two properties which the two triangles share (they will all have three sides!) and one property which makes them different. Ask five or six pupils who have drawn different triangles to come to the whiteboard and draw their triangles on the whiteboard. Give each pair 3 minutes to think of as many properties of these triangles as they can. You can use this activity to model the mathematical vocabulary which you want the pupils to draw on in the activity.

Represent the problem: the pupils should decide on different ways to represent the classification of the triangles that they use. They will need to take care in labelling their diagrams and you may want to act as scribe for this part of the activity. Some pupils may want to take photographs of their sorting rather than trying to redraw all the triangles. They could make labels to go alongside their groups.

Developing mathematical thinking and reasoning and communicating learning: the discussion focusing on describing properties of the triangles and noticing similarities and differences by exploring their properties is an important part of developing mathematical thinking. The activity also provides pupils with a reason to communicate their thinking, which supports them in developing an appropriate mathematical vocabulary.

Recording: this is another activity which lends itself to creating wall displays. Each group can choose one of the ways of classifying the triangles and create a wall poster which incorporates the names of all the triangles.

Possible developments: the pupils could create a similar activity for other shapes such as quadrilaterals or simple 3D shapes.

Skills developed:

- recognising and naming common 2D shapes
- identifying and describing the properties of 2D shapes, including the number of sides and line symmetry in a vertical line
- comparing and sorting common 2D shapes.

Task 8.4 Folding and cutting

Take a piece of A4 paper.

Make one fold anywhere on the paper.

Make a cut so that you create two different shapes.

Sketch the two shapes that you have made and name them.

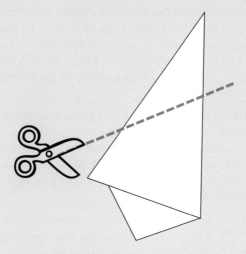

Can you find ways to fold the paper so that you make:

- a square
- a rhombus
- a parallelogram
- a trapezium
- a kite?

Target group: Y5/6/Stages 5 and 6.

Resources: scissors; plenty of A4 paper. Start the activity with scrap paper. Use coloured paper for pupils to choose one shape to make for the final display.

Possible starting point: you may choose to model the activity. Make a fold which is not perpendicular to any of the sides and then draw a possible line along which you will cut. Ask pupils to discuss in pairs the shapes that they think will be made when you make the cut and unfold the pieces. Name the shapes that you make and discuss their properties.

Representing and recording the problem: pupils can sketch the folds and the cut lines and then sketch the shapes that are made. This will help them as they explore the different shapes that can be made. Encourage pupils to refer back to the drawings when they try to create different shapes.

Developing mathematical thinking and reasoning: pupils are developing their visualisation skills during this activity. They have to imagine the shapes that will be made before they make the cut. Encourage the pupils to explain their thinking. Refer them back to previous attempts so that they are drawing on their prior experience.

Communicating learning: during a plenary session ask pupils to describe how they visualised the shapes that they were trying to make. What was their thinking process when they tried to make a kite or a trapezium for example? They should discuss their 'failures' and their mistaken assumptions as well as their successes and 'aha' moments. What errors did they make in their visualisation and how did they learn from these errors?

Possible developments: this can be developed using different sizes of pieces of paper and different numbers of cuts. What happens if you make two cuts? What about two folds and one cut? And so on.

Skills developed:

- distinguishing between regular and irregular polygons based on reasoning about equal sides and angles
- identifying and describing properties of quadrilaterals (including the parallelogram, rhombus and trapezium), and classifying using parallel sides, equal sides, equal angles
- using the term 'diagonal' and making conjectures about the angles formed between sides, and between diagonals and parallel sides, and other properties of quadrilaterals
- comparing and classifying geometric shapes based on their properties and sizes and finding unknown angles in any triangles, quadrilaterals and regular polygons
- identifying and describing properties of triangles and classifying as isosceles, equilateral or scalene
- recognising reflective and rotational symmetry in regular polygons
- explaining methods and justifying reasoning orally and in writing
- making hypotheses and testing them out.

Task 8.5 Lines of symmetry

Draw all the lines of symmetry on the letters of the alphabet.

ABCDEF
GHIJKLM
NOPQRST
UVWXYZ

Which letters have rotational symmetry?

Can you think of any words which have line symmetry?

Target group: Y3/4/Stages 3 and 4.

Resources: a sheet with all the letters of the alphabet; mini whiteboards.

Possible starting point: write your name on the board. Ask a pupil to come to the board and draw any line of symmetry on any of the letters (if no letters in your name have a line of symmetry use an alternative name).

Ask pupils to write their own name on a whiteboard (using all upper case letters). They should pass their whiteboard to a partner who should look for lines of symmetry. They can then check each other's solutions.

Representing and recording the problem: the pupils can group the letters into those that do have line symmetry and those that don't. They can do the same for rotational symmetry. They can sketch each orientation of any letter with rotational symmetry (H and X).

Developing mathematical thinking and reasoning: ask the pupils to describe how they are visualising the lines of symmetry. Try to get them to articulate their own definitions of line symmetry and rotational symmetry.

Communicating learning: encourage the pupils to articulate their reasoning to you and to the other pupils in their group. Ask them how they know that a shape has symmetry. How can they be sure that a letter does not have symmetry?

Possible developments: explore symmetry in the environment: either in the classroom or even better outdoors. Take photographs to create a display.

Skills developed:

- identifying and sketching lines of symmetry in 2D shapes and patterns
- finding examples of shapes and symmetry in the environment and in art
- recognising line symmetry in a variety of diagrams, including where the line of symmetry does not dissect the original shape.

Task 8.6 Shapes in a bag

You should work in groups of four or five on this activity. Each group will have a bag with some shapes in it. Take it in turns to put your hand in the bag. Describe the shape that you are holding. The first person who guesses the shape correctly and uses the correct name has the next turn.

Replace the 2D shapes with 3D shapes and play the game again.

Target group: Y1/2/Stages 1 and 2.

Resources: sets of 2D and 3D shapes; bags to place the shapes in (enough sets of these for the pupils to work in groups of three or four). You should include regular and irregular shapes.

Possible starting point: play the game with the whole class initially. Use the pupils to describe the shapes although you can take the opportunity to model the mathematical vocabulary that you want the pupils to use.

Representing and recording the problem: after the activity is completed the pupils can sketch the shapes and list the properties they used to describe each shape along with the name of each shape. You could also make a table display using the 3D shapes which includes labels of the shapes, properties and their names.

Developing mathematical thinking and reasoning: this activity supports the development of visualisation skills as the pupils have to visualise the shape that they are feeling in the bag. It also asks the pupils to focus on properties which make each shape unique. This usually means that they will have to consider several properties before the shape can be guessed.

Communicating learning: ask the pupils to describe which properties made it easy to describe a shape and which did not describe shapes uniquely. For example, just giving the numbers of sides may not give the unique shape.

Possible developments: pupils can describe a shape that they have drawn so that a partner can draw exactly the same shape on their mini whiteboard (shapes which are exactly the same are called congruent).

Skills developed:

- recognising and naming common 2D shapes, for example, rectangles (including squares), circles and triangles
- recognising and naming common 3D shapes, for example, cuboids (including cubes), pyramids and spheres
- identifying and describing the properties of 2D shapes, including the number of sides and line symmetry in a vertical line
- identifying and describing the properties of 3D shapes, including the number of edges, vertices and faces
- identifying 2D shapes on the surface of 3D shapes, for example, a circle on a cylinder and a triangle on a pyramid
- comparing and sorting common 2D and 3D shapes and everyday objects.

Task 8.7 Shapes out of cubes

Can you build these shapes using interlocking cubes?

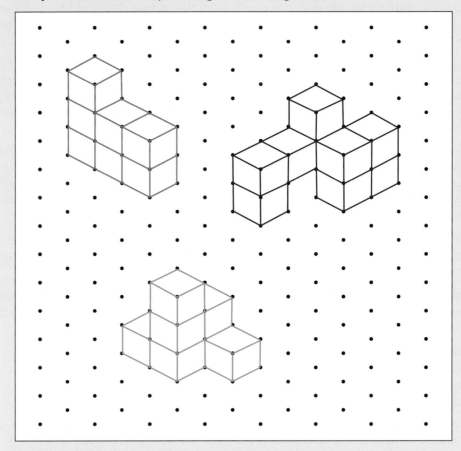

Try to find more than one way to build each shape. Some of the cubes may be hidden.

Make a shape using five interlocking cubes. Sketch it on isometric paper. Give the sketch to a friend. Can they make your shape using the sketch?

How many different shapes can you make out of five interlocking cubes?

Target group: Y5/6/Stages 5 and 6.

Resources: interlocking cubes, isometric paper.

Possible starting point: ask a pupil to come to the front and describe a shape that you have made with four cubes. Do this cube by cube so that the pupil has to gradually build up the shape. After every instruction check with the whole class that the pupil is following the instructions accurately. If there are choices to be made revisit the choices after the next instruction to check that the shape is being built correctly. When the shape is complete show the class how to draw the shape using isometric paper. Draw a set of dots on the whiteboard so that you can model it on the whiteboard.

Ask pupils to repeat this activity using five cubes each. They should then work in pairs to sketch their shapes on isometric paper.

Representing and recording the problem: using the isometric paper might be challenging as pupils may not have learned this technique. Allow pupils several attempts as they may well not get it right first time. Encourage pupils to look at the shapes in different orientations so that they can 'see' the shape in the orientation which they are sketching it in.

Developing mathematical thinking and reasoning: ask pupils to describe their reasoning aloud to elicit their understanding and to allow them to better articulate their own understanding. The purpose of the hidden cubes is to allow several possible solutions. In convincing themselves and then convincing you that their solution is accurate pupils are developing their mathematical thinking and reasoning. As with many of the activities in this chapter the key skill of 'visualisation' is at the heart of the activity.

Communicating learning: the opening activity asks pupils to be precise in their descriptions of the shapes that they are building. The 'hidden' cubes in the drawings also mean that pupils have to be careful in their descriptions of position.

Possible developments: pupils can be shown how to draw plan views and side and front elevations as an alternative way of recording 3D shapes. In fact this is a more accurate way of recording as only one possible shape can be represented by these three views.

Skills developed:

- identifying 3D shapes, including cubes and other cuboids, from 2D representations
- recognising, describing and building simple 3D shapes
- recognising the relationships between different 2D and 3D shapes
- visualising and describing the properties of 3D shapes, e.g. faces, edges and vertices.

Task 8.6 Making bunting

You are going to make bunting to go around the classroom for a party. You will use large sheets of sugar paper to make the 'flags' and garden twine to attach them together.

Calculate how many sheets of sugar paper you will need to create enough flags to go around the room.

What length of twine will you need?

Target group: Year 3/4/Stages 3 and 4.

Resources: large sheets of sugar paper, garden twine, scissors, measuring equipment.

Possible starting point: this is best used as a practical activity when you actually need to prepare the classroom for a party. You could choose to decorate a hall or an outdoor space. The important thing is that it becomes a real-life problem with real-life outcomes. Encourage groups to explore the different sorts of triangles that can be used for the bunting and to experiment with the twine to see how much it will 'hang' between the fixed points.

Represent the problem: pupils should be encouraged to sketch out their solutions before actually making the bunting and cutting the twine. It may be appropriate for groups to present their solutions to the whole class before embarking on making the bunting. They should explore different angles at the base of the triangles (which may well be isosceles). They need to be aesthetically pleasing as well as an efficient use of paper.

Developing mathematical thinking and reasoning and communicating learning: this is best developed through a presentation of the solution. It is particularly effective for groups to vote on the 'best' solution as this encourages all the groups to take care over their presentation. It also focuses groups on the criteria they are using for assessing the 'best' solution.

Recording: the presentation offers a good opportunity for groups to record both their thought process and the final solution to the problem.

Possible developments: this activity could form a part of a cross-curricular piece of mathematics around planning a party. There are opportunities for measuring and ratio if you make refreshments and for budgeting if you are raising money for charity.

Skills developed:

- drawing 2D shapes using given dimensions and angles
- knowing angles are measured in degrees; estimating and comparing acute, obtuse and reflex angles
- estimating, recognising and drawing angles and using a protractor to measure to the nearest degree
- identifying and describing properties of triangles and classifying as isosceles, equilateral or scalene
- making, testing and refining hypotheses
- explaining and justifying methods, reasoning, strategies, results or conclusions orally.

CHAPTER 9
MEASUREMENT

The activities in this chapter develop some of the tasks and resource ideas from Chapter 8 in *Understanding and Teaching Mathematics* which helped you develop your own understanding of measurement. The activities here should help you explore measurement with the pupils that you are working with. There is a particular focus on conservation and comparison of measure, and on units of measurement and reading scales.

Each activity has been designed in the same way as all the activities in the book. On one page there is a task sheet you can use with your pupils. These are available to download from the companion website. On the facing page there is a prompt sheet for you. As in the previous chapter this details:

- the target group for the task
- resources you will need
- possible starting points
- ways to represent the problem
- prompts to support you in developing mathematical thinking and reasoning
- prompts to support learners in communicating their learning
- prompts for recording: things to look for and encourage
- possible developments and alternative routes through the problem
- the mathematical skills that pupils will develop whilst engaged on the task.

Make sure that you try out these tasks yourself or with colleagues so that you feel confident in your own measurement skills when you introduce them to your pupils. If you are reading or have read the companion volume *Understanding and Teaching Primary Mathematics* you may have already worked through many of these activities.

I would encourage you to be flexible. This way the pupils will discover things that you hadn't thought of. Don't be alarmed – be excited! Follow them on their new points of departure and enjoy learning about measurement together.

Task 9.1 What measurements do you know?

Try to complete this table with objects around the classroom or at home. For the very small or very large measures you may need to do some research on the internet or make estimates.

These objects measure:

Length	
1mm	
1cm	
1m	
1km	
10km	
100km	

These objects weigh:

Mass	
1mg	
1g	
1kg	
10kg	
100kg	

These things hold:

Capacity	
1ml	
10ml	
500ml	
1l	
100l	

Target group: Year 3/4/Stages 3 and 4.

Resources: lots of measuring equipment; access to the internet or reference books for research.

Possible starting point: there is a fantastic YouTube clip called 'The smallest to the biggest thing in the universe' which makes a great starting point for this activity (see www.youtube.com/watch?v=EMLPJqeW78Q). Alternatively, bring in some interesting facts about very large or very small things. There are also many versions of the game 'Top Trumps' which include facts about measurement. A possible starting point would be playing the game of Top Trumps in small groups and discussing interesting facts that came out of the game.

Representing and recording the problem: it is interesting to try to draw some graphics which show the relative size of some of the objects from the video. These can be drawn to scale as the scale factor is always a multiple of 10.

Developing mathematical thinking and reasoning and communicating learning: this activity allows pupils to bring their own experience of measurement into the classroom. It supports them in developing an understanding of units of measurement in terms of objects that they can visualise. This is very helpful when estimating measurement. We need to start from something we know in order to estimate the measurement of something that we don't know.

Possible developments: pupils can explore very small or very large objects and develop graphics which show comparisons. The NRich website (https://nrich. maths.org/7753) outlines an activity which explores a model of the universe using spherical objects and sheets of toilet paper.

Skills developed:

- choosing and using standard metric units and their abbreviations (km, m, cm, mm, kg, g, l and ml) when estimating, measuring and recording length, weight and capacity
- knowing and using the relationships between familiar units of length, mass and capacity
- knowing the meaning of 'kilo', 'centi' and 'milli'
- converting between different units of measure.

Task 9.2 Which is the heaviest?

Look at these different sized boxes. Try to put them in order of weight without picking them up. Then use a pair of balance scales to see if you were correct.

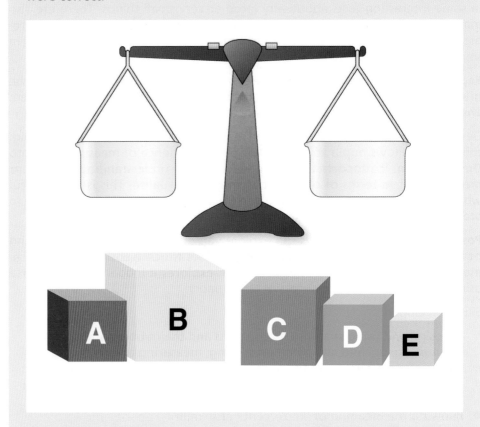

Use the balance scales and some weights to weigh the objects.

Target group: Y1/2/Stages 1 and 2.

Resources: balance scales, weights, five boxes of different sizes. Carefully place objects in the boxes so that the largest box (by volume) is not the heaviest box. The aim of this activity is to show pupils that size (by volume or length) is not directly proportionate to weight.

Possible starting point: I often use this activity as a whole class activity. Alternatively, it could be one activity in a circus of activities all exploring conservation, for example you could also look at conservation of volume using different containers and water.

Representing and recording the problem: label the boxes A, B, C, D and E (if there are five!) and ask pupils to write down the labels in order of weight. They also need to create a table to record the weights. You could use standard weights or some non-standard weights (such as cubes). This depends on the stage of learning that the pupils have reached. Pupils can also use the > and < signs to show the relative weights of pairs or triads of boxes.

Developing mathematical thinking and reasoning and communicating learning: this activity supports pupils in coming to a better understanding of the conservation of measurements. They also begin to understand the importance of using standard units to make comparisons.

Possible developments: as I suggested above this activity would link well to other activities exploring the conservation of measurement. Another development would be to move on to looking at standard units.

Skills developed:

- estimating, measuring and comparing weights and capacities, choosing and using suitable uniform non-standard and standard units and appropriate measuring instruments
- comparing, describing and solving practical problems for: mass/weight (for example, heavy/light, heavier than, lighter than); capacity and volume (for example, full/empty, more than, less than, half, half full, quarter)
- measuring and beginning to record: mass/weight, capacity and volume
- choosing and using appropriate standard units to estimate and measure mass (kg/g); capacity (litres/ml) to the nearest appropriate unit; using scales and measuring vessels
- comparing and ordering mass, volume/capacity and recording the results using >, < and =.

Task 9.3 Area and perimeter

Explorers in a field are each given 100m of rope and four stakes. Each explorer uses the four stakes and the rope to section off a piece of land which they will dig in order to find gold. What are the dimensions of the shape that they make to enclose the largest area they can?

Target group: Y3/4 Stages 3 and 4.

Resources: squared paper or mini whiteboards which have square grids so that pupils can explore lots of different shapes; string and pegs.

Possible starting point: this activity is best when the introduction is kept to a minimum. Pupils may think that all the shapes will have the same area but it is better that they realise there are many different areas for themselves. I usually use all attainment small groups for this activity as a wide range of prior experience will allow the groups to think more widely around the problem.

Represent the problem: pupils may find it helpful at first to use string and pegs to model the problem. Then they can form different shapes to explore, using the squared paper, to help them calculate the areas.

Developing mathematical thinking and reasoning and communicating learning: as well as working with the misconception that all shapes with a given perimeter have the same area and vice versa this activity helps pupils see the importance of systematic recording. They will need to draw on the experience they are gaining throughout the activity to explore the types of shapes that are giving them the largest area.

Recording: this activity lends itself to final presentations. Each group can represent a different mining company all presenting their solution to the problem. The whole class then acts as a 'consortium' to agree which solution they would adopt as company policy. Groups have to draw on their learning to present a convincing rationale for their solution. These 'formal' presentations can form the record of the learning.

Possible developments: a sensible development is to explore the range of perimeters that can be made with a fixed area. One way of exploring this is by using carpet tiles. If you have 20 carpet tiles all of which are $1m^2$ what are the different possible perimeters that can be made?

Skills developed:

- measuring and calculating the perimeter of a rectilinear figure (including squares) in centimetres and metres
- finding the area of rectilinear shapes by counting squares
- explaining methods and reasoning orally, including initial thoughts about possible answers to a problem.

Task 9.4 Choosing and using appropriate units

Work in pairs. Talk about and write down objects that you would use these units to measure.

Unit	Object
kilometre	
metre	
centimetre	
millimetre	
tonne	
kilogram	
gram	
milligram	
litre	
centilitre	
millilitre	
degrees Celcius	

Sometimes we measure using 'imperial units'.

Write sentences which include the following units:

1 miles (in the UK and the USA distance is measured in miles; a kilometre is 5/8 of a mile)
2 feet
3 inches
4 pounds
5 ounces
6 Fahrenheit.

Target group: Y3/4/Stages 3 and 4.

Resources: no need for any resources although access to the internet or the library for research would be helpful.

Possible starting point: this is another activity that can be started using the 'Top Trumps' card game. Many of these packs contain measurements of different kinds. Collect different sets so that you can use them for a wide range of measurements. Alternatively, you could use some facts that you have researched – the longest cycle ride, the tallest building, the lightest animal and so on.

Representing and recording the problem: there is no need to develop the recording of this problem beyond completing the table.

Developing mathematical thinking and reasoning: this activity allows learners to draw on their own experience and interests to understand the appropriate units of measurement to use. If learners attach units to things that they are interested in or that they have knowledge of they will be able to remember which units to apply to which measurement.

Communicating learning: the pairs can share their results. It may be useful to ask the class to pick the object which best represents each unit so that you can create a poster for a wall display.

Possible developments: groups could research facts about animals and prepare a presentation. The presentation could include facts such as:

- My animal weighs ...
- My animal measures ...
- My animal can run/fly/swim at ...

Skills developed:

- choosing and using appropriate units and equipment to estimate, measure and record measurements
- knowing the relationship between kilometres and metres, metres and centimetres, kilograms and grams, litres and millilitres.

Task 9.5 True/false/iffy

Decide if these statements are always true, sometimes true or never true.

Design a poster for each statement which shows why your answer is correct.

1 If you double the dimensions of a rectangle you double the length of the perimeter.
2 If you double the dimensions of a rectangle the area doubles.
3 If you double the length of the longest sides of a rectangle but leave the width the same you double the area.
4 If you double the dimensions of a cuboid you double the volume.

Target group: Y5/6/Stages 5 and 6.

Resources: Squared paper for drafting; large pieces of sugar paper for posters.

Possible starting point: you should allow groups to explore these questions with very little initial input. You can check that pupils remember the terms area, perimeter and volume as you move round the groups once they have started. I often choose to have groups work on one of the statements each. Then they can share their results at the end. You may want to ask for an intuitive response at the beginning of the lesson that you can come back to when the groups have worked on the statements.

Representing and recording the problem: pupils should sketch diagrams which show examples of the rectangles and cuboids they use to exemplify their solution. Encourage pupils to draw these to scale so that the posters are accurate. They may need to use isometric paper for the cuboids.

Developing mathematical thinking and reasoning: this activity works with common misconceptions. It also helps pupils understand why area is measured in square units (we are multiplying two dimensions together) and volume in cubic units (we are multiplying three dimensions together).

Communicating learning: encourage different groups to present their solutions to the whole class at the end. The pupils can then make links between the different statements that they have explored and check each other's conclusions.

Possible developments: pupils can explore other similar relationships. What happens if we multiply dimensions by 3 or 4 for example.

Skills developed:

- measuring and calculating the perimeter of composite rectilinear shapes in centimetres and metres
- calculating and comparing the area of rectangles (including squares), including using standard units, square centimetres (cm^2) and square metres (m^2); and estimating the area of irregular shapes.

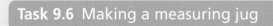

Task 9.6 Making a measuring jug

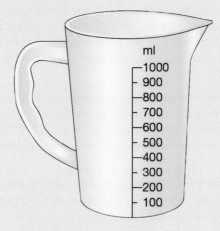

Make your own measuring jug using an old water bottle and containers which hold 50ml and 100ml.

Target group: Y3/4/Stages 3 and 4.

Resources: enough water bottles for one per group; a selection of containers that you have calibrated so that the pupils can measure 50ml and 100ml.

Possible starting point: describe the task to the pupils and arrange them in all attainment groups. This activity benefits from having groups with a wide range of prior experience. Ask pairs to discuss how they might carry out the activity and share these ideas before the groups begin the task.

Representing and recording the problem: the pupils will need permanent markers to create the scales on the sides of the water bottles. Encourage them to sketch the solutions before they start on the task.

Developing mathematical thinking and reasoning: this activity allows pupils to develop a good sense of what 50ml and 100ml 'look like' as well as a good sense of 1l. The water bottles that you use should hold at least 1l.

Communicating learning: at the end of the activity groups should share their solutions. Encourage pupils to focus on the process and how they decided to go about the task. They should also check the scales that they have created by using a calibrated measuring jug at the end of the lesson.

Possible developments: pupils can create other measuring devices – metre rules, scales, by using a set of standard units.

Skills developed:

- measuring, comparing, adding and subtracting: lengths (m/cm/mm); mass (kg/g); volume/capacity (l/ml)
- knowing and using the relationships between familiar units of length, mass and capacity; knowing the meanings of 'kilo', 'centi' and 'milli'
- understanding everyday systems of measurement in length, weight, capacity.

Task 9.7 Telling the time

This clock is showing 3:45pm. Write down all the ways that you could say this time.

Here are some answers that another group gave me. Explain what is wrong with each of these statements.

- It is 45 minutes to 4.
- It is 9:20pm.
- It is 9 minutes to 4.
- It is 9 minutes past 3.
- It is 18 minutes past nine.
- It is 03:45.
- It is 13:45.

Make up another question like this for the rest of your class to answer.

Target group: Y1/2/Stages 1 and 2.

Resources: analogue clocks with moveable hands; blank clock faces to draw hands on.

Possible starting point: ask the pupils for times that they know. For example the time that they come to school, the time that they break for lunch, the time that they go to bed. Model this on a clock and ask them for all the different ways that you could say this time.

Representing and recording the problem: pupils need clock faces to draw the times on when they come to set their own question. These are available to download from the companion website. You may need to act as scribe for some of the groups. Alternatively, make sure that each group has a confident writer in the group who can take responsibility for writing down the questions that they come up with.

Developing mathematical thinking and reasoning: move around the groups to hear their responses to the incorrect times. This activity deals with a wide range of misconceptions and you, or a teaching assistant if you have one, need to try to hear as many of the responses as you can. You can refer pupils back to these errors when they are creating their own poster. See if they can reproduce each 'error'. They may also be able to find a few misconceptions of their own.

Communicating learning: each group should prepare a poster with a similar task on it. These can either be shared with other groups or you can work on two or three of the posters with the whole class.

Possible developments: ask the pupils to take the problems that they have created home to work on with their parents or carers.

Skills developed:

- telling and writing the time to five minutes, including quarter past/to the hour and drawing the hands on a clock face to show these times
- telling and writing the time from an analogue clock, including using Roman numerals from I to XII, and 12-hour and 24-hour clocks
- estimating and reading time with increasing accuracy to the nearest minute
- reading, writing and converting time between analogue and digital 12- and 24-hour clocks
- using am, pm and 12-hour digital clock notation.

Task 9.8 More than 1kg; less than 1kg

Make a collection of objects and complete this table.

Objects			
Weigh less than 100g			
Weigh between 100g and 500g			
Weigh between 500g and 1kg			
Weigh more than 1kg			

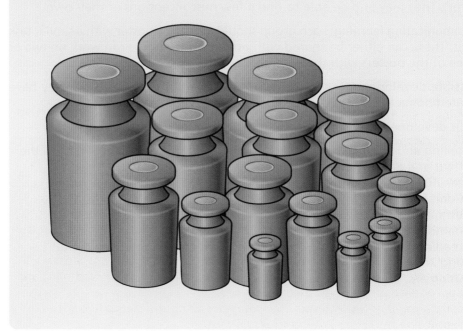

Target group: Y1/2/Stages 1 and 2.

Resources: scales; large collection of objects – it is best if these are brought into school by the pupils. Alternatively, you could go out for a walk to collect them.

Possible starting point: select one of the objects and ask pupils to estimate the mass of the object. Pupils should work in pairs on this. Compare pupils' estimates using the scales. Repeat this activity so that pupils can draw on the experience to make a better estimate for the second object. Pupils should work in all attainment groups on this activity as they will benefit from having a wide range of prior experience in the groups.

Representing and recording the problem: pupils may want to create another table which lists the objects in order of mass with their estimates and the actual mass next to each other so that they can see how their estimates became more accurate as the activity progressed (hopefully!). This can also be represented by putting the objects on a table and making labels.

Developing mathematical thinking and reasoning and communicating learning: this encourages pupils to develop their skill of estimating as they use a range of objects. It also allows them to develop a 'sense' of 100g, 500g and 1kg.

Possible developments: pupils can repeat this activity for different units of measurement. For example:

- shorter than 10cm, between 10cm and 50cm, between 50cm and 1m, longer than 1m
- takes less than 10 seconds, takes between 10 seconds and 30 seconds, takes between 30 seconds and a minute, takes longer than 1 minute
- holds less than 100ml, holds between 100ml and 500ml, holds between 500ml and 1l, holds more than 1l.

Skills developed:

- choosing and using appropriate standard units to estimate and measure length/height in any direction (m/cm); mass (kg/g); temperature (°C); capacity (litres/ml) to the nearest appropriate unit, using rulers, scales, thermometers and measuring vessels
- comparing and ordering lengths, mass, volume/capacity and recording the results using >, < and =
- estimating, measuring and comparing lengths, weights and capacities, choosing and using suitable uniform non-standard and standard units and appropriate measuring instruments
- comparing lengths, weights and capacities using the standard units: centimetre, metre, gram, kilogram and litre.

Task 9.9 Teddy bears picnic

You are going to have a teddy bears picnic. Collect some teddy bears.

Make plates and bowls for them and make some spoons.

Make chairs that will be comfortable for them to sit in.

Make a shelter for them in case it rains at the picnic.

Target group: Y1/2/Stages 1 and 2.

Resources: teddy bears of all different sizes, cardboard and card for making plates and bowls; empty boxes to make chairs and the shelters.

Possible starting point: this activity is best carried out in a home corner as a part of a circus of activities. Once the picnic has been set up the children can return and make more utensils and food for the picnic. Children will enjoy returning to the activity and engaging in talk about the things that they are making.

Representing and recording the problem: this is a practical activity so I would not expect the children to be drawing or writing anything. I would expect them to be talking mathematically and the main role for the teacher is to encourage this mathematical talk. Pupils should be encouraged to make utensils and containers and then 'check' that they are the right size for the teddy bears. If they decide that they are too big or too small they should make the item again.

Developing mathematical thinking and reasoning and communicating learning: use the language of comparison to develop the children's mathematical thinking and encourage them to describe to you what they are making and how they are deciding how big it should be. What prior experience are they drawing on? When they make the shelters how do they decide what the dimensions of the shelter should be? What uniform, non-standard measures do they use?

Recording: the best way to record this activity is through photographs. Take photographs of the children engaged in the activity. Annotate the photographs with examples of the mathematical talk that the children were engaged in.

Possible developments: building shelters is an excellent activity to explore measurement with young children. Find other animals that the children can build shelters for from very small animals to large imaginary animals.

Skills developed:

- comparing, describing and solving practical problems for lengths and heights (for example, long/short, longer/shorter, tall/short, double/half); mass or weight (for example, heavy/light, heavier than, lighter than); capacity and volume (for example, full/empty, more than, less than, half, half full, quarter)
- measuring and beginning to record the following: lengths and heights; mass/weight; capacity and volume.

Task 9.10 Cereal boxes

You need a cereal box for this activity.

How much cereal does your box hold?

Design a box with different dimensions that will hold the same amount of cereal.

Choose a name for your cereal.

Design a logo that will fit on the new box you have designed.

You should draw this logo on the net of the box.

Target group: Y5/6/Stages 5 and 6.

Resources: cereal boxes of different dimensions. You may also want to use uniform non-standard measures such as unit cubes.

Possible starting point: ask pupils to estimate the capacity of their boxes. They should then use unit cubes to see how close their estimate was. Pupils will often underestimate the capacity considerably. Pupils should then work on the activity in all attainment groups. The groups will benefit from being made up of learners with a wide range of prior experience.

Represent the problem: pupils should open up the boxes to understand the shape of the net. They will then need to make decisions about the shape and size of the new net. They should sketch these ideas before they make them. It may be the case that groups need to make several new boxes before they are happy with the result.

Developing mathematical thinking and reasoning and communicating learning: pupils are developing the ability to visualise the ways in which nets make cuboids. This visualising of 2D and 3D shapes is an important skill. They are also gaining a 'sense' of capacity. Many people only have a limited idea of what $100cm^3$ 'looks like' for example.

Recording: groups should prepare a presentation for the whole class. This activity is great for peer assessment. Peers can give feedback on each presentation and select a new design that they think is the most appropriate. Encourage feedback along the 'two stars and a wish' format so that the focus is on the positive.

Possible developments: ask pupils to design packages for unusually shaped objects or packages to hold standard objects such as stock cubes. All of these activities give a good sense of the units of capacity and volume.

Skills developed:

- measuring and calculating the perimeter of composite rectilinear shapes in centimetres and metres
- calculating and comparing the area of rectangles (including squares), including using standard units, square centimetres (cm^2) and square metres (m^2) and estimating the area of irregular shapes
- estimating volume, for example, using $1cm^3$ blocks to build cuboids (including cubes) and capacity, for example, using water.

CHAPTER 10
STATISTICS

The activities in this chapter develop some of the tasks and resource ideas from Chapter 10 in *Understanding and Teaching Mathematics* which helped you to develop your understanding of statistics and data handling. The activities here should help you explore statistics in your mathematics classrooms. Statistics involve the collection, representation and analysis of data to answer questions. This process often throws up new questions that we need to answer.

Each activity in this book has been designed in the same way. On one page there is a task sheet you can use with your pupils. These are available to download from the companion website. On the facing page there is a prompt sheet for you. As in the previous chapter this details:

- the target group for the task
- resources you will need
- possible starting points
- ways to represent the problem
- prompts to support you in developing mathematical thinking and reasoning
- prompts to support learners in communicating their learning
- prompts for recording: things to look for and encourage
- possible developments and alternative routes through the problem
- the mathematical skills that pupils will develop whilst engaged on the task.

Make sure that you try out these tasks yourself or with colleagues so that you feel confident working with statistics and data handling when you introduce the activities to your pupils. If you are reading or have read the companion volume *Understanding and Teaching Primary Mathematics* you may have already worked through many of these activities.

Allow the pupils to develop the ideas flexibly – if they discover things that you hadn't thought of don't be alarmed – be excited! Follow them on their new points of departure and enjoy learning statistics together.

Task 10.1 What does this data mean?

Look at this column graph.

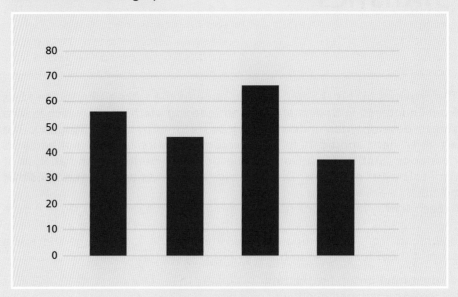

Think of three different sets of data that this graph could represent.

Redraw the graph with labelled axes.

Write down three facts about the data.

Think of another question that you could ask based on this data.

Carry out research that helps you answer this question.

Target group: Y3/4/Stages 3 and 4.

Resources: access to research materials or the web for research; squared paper to sketch the graph.

Possible starting point: find a graph or a chart that is in the news. Show this on the whiteboard without the headings and ask pupils to work in pairs to think what the chart might represent. After you have taken an idea from each pair show the class what the chart actually represents. Discuss the text that goes with the chart to see if the newspaper has accurately interpreted the data. I would suggest all attainment groups for this activity so that there will be a range of interests within each group.

Representing and recording the problem: the focus here is redrawing the chart so that the axes contain the necessary information. Then when the groups have collected data to answer their own question they will need to decide what form of graph or chart is the most appropriate. Encourage the pupils to discuss this at some length before they decide which chart will be best to illustrate their data.

Developing mathematical thinking and reasoning: the starting point for this activity is interpreting data. This is a way of starting the data handling cycle in a different place so that the initial focus can be interpretation rather than collection. This also leads into the pupils asking their own question. This should be something that they are interested in themselves and so they will be motivated to carry out the data collection and analysis.

Communicating learning: each group should present their findings to the rest of the class. It is useful to use peer assessment and evaluation at this point. You could use the 'two stars and a wish' process.

Possible developments: pupils can look in the newspapers and on the television news for charts and graphs and critically analyse the stories that run alongside the graphs and charts.

Skills developed:

- interpreting and presenting discrete and continuous data using appropriate graphical methods
- answering a question by identifying what data to collect; organising, presenting and interpreting data in tables, diagrams, tally charts, frequency tables, pictograms (symbol representing 2, 5, 10 or 20 units) and bar charts (intervals labelled in 2s, 5s, 10s or 20s)
- comparing the impact of representations where scales have different intervals.

Task 10.2 Mini Olympics

There are three events in our mini Olympics

Event 1: How far can people in your class jump from a standing start?

Event 2: How many times can people throw and catch a ball in one minute?

Event 3: How many times can people in your class jump up and down in one minute?

Target group: Y5/6/Stages 5 and 6.

Resources: measuring tapes, stopwatches, tennis balls, masking tape to make start of jumps, large squared paper to record results, felt tips, marker pens.

Possible starting point: show a record-breaking clip from YouTube, for example the world record 'broad jump' (www.youtube.com/watch?v=n0UeHxglMJ4). Ask pupils to work in pairs to discuss how they can make sure that each event is fair. Agree as a class how they will organise each event so that the results are fair. Relate this to the idea of fair testing. The class can either work in three large groups – one on each event, or six groups with two groups covering each event.

Representing and recording the problem: each group should decide how they are going to record the results from their event. They need time to think about this before they start collecting the data. Every member of the class should take part in each event to give a large set of data. Once the data is collected the group then needs to decide how best to illustrate the data. Again, they will need time to think about the different ways that they can illustrate the data. Encourage pupils to use measures such as mean, median and mode to describe their data. You should also point out the difference between discrete data (catching a ball and jumping) and continuous data (the long jump). This means that they will need to decide on suitable intervals for the long jump measurements.

Developing mathematical thinking and reasoning: the pupils are making their own decisions about how to ensure that the 'tests' are fair and are also making decisions about the collection and representation of the data. This develops their understanding and awareness of the data handling cycle.

Communicating learning: each group should present their findings to the rest of the class. It is useful to use peer assessment and evaluation at this point. You could use the 'two stars and a wish' process. You may choose to have an awards ceremony for each event.

Possible developments: the class could use the skills that they have developed to run the school sports day and collect and interpret all of the data that this would provide. Alternatively, they could explore the wealth of data on athletics that is available on the web.

Skills developed:

- answering a set of related questions by collecting, selecting and organising relevant data; drawing conclusions from their own and others' data and identifying further questions to ask
- drawing and interpreting frequency tables, pictograms and bar line charts, with the vertical axis labelled for example in 2s, 5s, 10s, 20s or 100s and considering the effect of changing the scale on the vertical axis
- calculating and interpreting the mean as an average.

Task 10.3 How do you get to school?

Look at these two ways of illustrating how pupils travel to school.

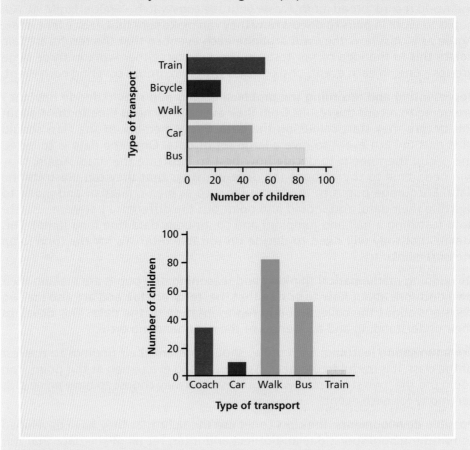

Write down the advantages and disadvantages of each way of illustrating the data.

Find out the different ways that pupils in your class travel to school.

Illustrate the data. Decide what type of graph or chart you will use to illustrate the data.

What does the data tell you about the methods used to travel to school?

What other questions would you like to ask about how people travel to your school?

Target group: Y5/6/Stages 5 and 6.

Resources: squared paper to record results. Large sheets of paper are useful to share findings.

Possible starting point: use the initial task as a discussion starter with 'talk partners' at the beginning of the lesson. Emphasise that there isn't a 'correct' answer; it is a matter of choice. I would recommend using all attainment groups to carry out the survey of the class. This means that a range of prior experience is available to each group.

Representing and recording the problem: pupils need to make their own decisions about how best to collect the data and what type of chart or graph they will use to represent the data. Pupils could use Excel and the charts that are embedded in that program. This allows them to experiment with the range of charts that are available.

Developing mathematical thinking and reasoning: the pupils are making their own decisions about how to ensure that the 'tests' are fair and are also making decisions about the collection and representation of the data. This develops their understanding and awareness of the data handling cycle.

Communicating learning: each group should present their findings to the rest of the class. It is useful to use peer assessment and evaluation at this point. You could use the 'two stars and a wish' process.

Possible developments: pupils can follow up the questions that they have posed for themselves at the end of this session. This may include collecting data at a whole school level.

Skills developed:

- answering a set of related questions by collecting, selecting and organising relevant data; drawing conclusions from their own and others' data and identifying further questions to ask
- drawing and interpreting frequency tables, pictograms and bar line charts, with the vertical axis labelled for example in 2s, 5s, 10s, 20s or 100s and considering the effect of changing the scale on the vertical axis
- calculating and interpreting the mean, median and mode as averages.

Task 10.4 Shape sorting

Walk around the school or, if you can, go on a shape walk in the local area.

Collect all the shapes that you see. Do this either by taking photographs or by making sketches.

When you get back to the classroom sort the shapes that you have found using these Carroll diagrams.

	Symmetrical	Not symmetrical
More than 4 sides		
Not more than 4 sides		

	Regular	Not regular
More than 4 sides		
Not more than 4 sides		

Think of other ways to sort the shapes.

Target group: Y3/4/Stages 3 and 4.

Resources: digital cameras, sketch books, adult support to go on shape walk; Venn diagram and Carroll diagram templates.

Possible starting point: collecting the shapes from the environment is important. This gets pupils used to 'noticing' shapes in their everyday environment. Start by looking for shapes in the classroom. Ask pupils to use discussion partners to talk about all the different properties of the shapes that they can see.

Represent the problem: the pupils will need to print off the photographs that they have taken or refer to the sketches they have made. They will also need to use research materials to name the shapes. It is much better if the pupils find out the names of the shapes for themselves. This is a good habit for them to get into.

Developing mathematical thinking and reasoning: the main thinking that is being developed is 'noticing'. If the pupils get into the habit of noticing the shapes in their everyday environment they will begin to see the shapes that are all around them. They will also start to notice their properties and will want to find out the names of unusual shapes. They will be able to explore the similarities and differences in shapes through the focus on their properties.

Communicating learning: pupils can share each other's classifications perhaps using the rotating flip chart technique. This would mean each group would create a Carroll diagram on a large piece of paper. They would enter the shapes that they 'collected' and then pass the paper onto another group to add their shapes. This would continue until the whole class has contributed.

Recording: use the downloadable blank Carroll diagrams from the companion website. A Carroll diagram should always have the criteria 'Property' and 'Not property'.

Possible developments: use Venn diagrams for sorting the same shapes.

Skills developed:

- using Venn diagrams or Carroll diagrams to sort data and objects using two or three criteria.

Task 10.5 Number sorting

Walk around the school or, if you can, go on a number walk in the local area.

Collect all the numbers that you see. Do this either by taking photographs or by writing them down.

When you get back to the classroom sort the numbers that you have found using this Venn diagram.

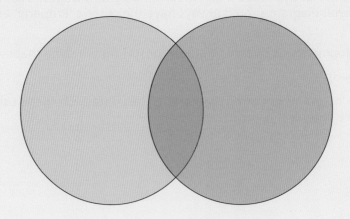

Target group: Y3/4/Stages 3 and 4.

Resources: digital cameras, sketch books, adult support to go on number walk; blank Venn diagram templates.

Possible starting point: collecting the numbers from the environment is important as this gets pupils used to 'noticing' numbers in their everyday environment. Start by looking for numbers around the classroom. Ask pupils to use discussion partners to talk about all the different properties of the numbers they have found.

Represent the problem: the pupils will need to print off the photographs that they have taken or to refer to their notebooks. They then will need to make decisions about which properties of numbers they will use to 'sort'.

Developing mathematical thinking and reasoning: the main thinking that is being developed is 'noticing'. If the pupils get into the habit of noticing numbers in their everyday environment they will begin to see the numbers that are all around them. They will also start to notice their properties and may find weird and wonderful properties of numbers.

Communicating learning: pupils can share each other's classifications perhaps using the rotating flip chart technique. This would mean one group would create a Venn diagram on a large piece of paper. They would enter the numbers that they 'collected' and then pass the paper onto another group to add their numbers. This would continue until the whole class has contributed.

Recording: you can download the Venn diagrams from the companion website.

Possible developments: use Carroll diagrams for sorting the same numbers.

Skills developed:

- using Venn diagrams or Carroll diagrams to sort data and objects.

Task 10.6 Mean, median, mode and range

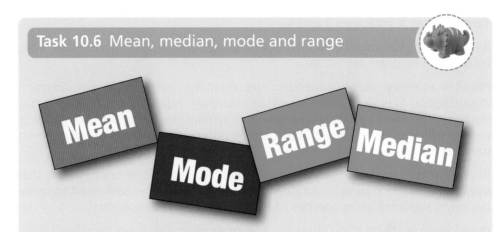

Can you find three sets of numbers for each of these properties:

1 six numbers with a mean of 6
2 eight numbers with a median of 4
3 ten numbers with a mode of 7.2
4 fifteen numbers with a range of 55?

Each set of numbers should represent something that you might find in a real-life context.

Target group: Y5/6/Stages 5 and 6.

Resources: no resources necessary. You can download the task sheet form the companion website.

Possible starting point: divide the class into four groups. Each group should explore one of the measures of 'spread'. They should both find a definition of their measure and an example of when they might use it in real life. This will help them when it comes to finding examples later in the session. Pupils should work on the task in pairs so that they can check each other's working and answers.

Representing the problem and developing mathematical thinking and reasoning: the important point about representation and reasoning here is that the pupils are constantly relating the measures back to real-life contexts in which they are used. This will help them remember the difference between the measures. They will also understand the methods for calculating the measures better by looking at the calculation from the endpoint rather than the starting point.

Communicating learning: working in pairs encourages pupils to communicate their thinking and consolidates their learning.

Recording: the pupils should record their answers in such a way that anyone reading their answers could follow their thinking. They can test this out by sharing their answers with other pairs of pupils.

Possible developments: look for examples of measures of spread in the newspapers or on the television news.

Skills developed:

- calculating and interpreting the range, mean, median and mode as averages.

Task 10.7 We like reading

Here is a statement for you:

'This class likes reading.'

How can you find out whether this statement is true?

What other facts about the reading habits of your classmates can you discover?

Target group: Y5/6/Stages 5 and 6.

Resources: none necessary.

Possible starting point: ask the pupils to sit in discussion pairs and talk about the statement 'The children in this class enjoy reading'. As part of this discussion they need to decide whether to vote for or against the statement. They need to talk about what is true about the statement and what is false. After five minutes' discussion time ask pairs to vote on the statement. Pick two or three people who voted 'yes' and ask them to give their reasons. Turn these reasons into questions which could be explored through a data handling exercise. Repeat for two or three people who voted 'no'. This should give you six questions which you can explore in more detail. Then divide the pupils into groups to explore each of the questions.

Representing and recording the problem: pupils need to make their own decisions about how best to collect the data and what type of chart or graph they will use to represent the data. Pupils could use Excel and the charts that are embedded in that program. This allows them to experiment with the range of charts that are available.

Developing mathematical thinking and reasoning: the pupils are making their own decisions about the collection and representation of the data. This develops their understanding and awareness of the data handling cycle.

Communicating learning: each group should present their findings to the rest of the class. It is useful to use peer assessment and evaluation at this point. You could use the 'two stars and a wish' process.

Possible developments: the activity could be extended to explore the reading habits of the whole school – including the teachers.

Skills developed:

- answering a set of related questions by collecting, selecting and organising relevant data; drawing conclusions from their own and others' data and identifying further questions to ask
- drawing and interpreting frequency tables, pictograms and bar line charts, with the vertical axis labelled for example in 2s, 5s, 10s, 20s or 100s and considering the effect of changing the scale on the vertical axis
- calculating and interpreting the mean, median and mode as averages.

Task 10.8 Human bar charts

Imagine your school was going to change the school dinners it served.

What advice would you give?

What meals would you like to see served at dinner time?

You are going to carry out a survey and then create a human bar chart to show the results.

Target group: Y3/4/Stages 3 and 4.

Resources: none necessary.

Possible starting point: this lesson can be carried out as a whole class lesson. It follows the same process as the Teachers TV clip that is available on the companion website. You should watch this clip before planning the lesson. The pupils should work in discussion pairs to talk through the meals they would like to see available for school dinners. They should also have a good reason for their choice. Then each pair should take it in turn to offer a suggestion. Select the six most popular suggestions. Ask pairs to discuss the best way to collect the data. You can then construct a data collection sheet.

Representing the problem: pupils should make copies of the data collection sheet and then small groups can visit different classes around the school so that they are collecting whole school data. This will mean that they will need to scale the axes on the 'human bar chart'. Create a scale either on a door or on one of the pupils as in the clip. Six pupils should then gradually lift up the image of their dish so that they create a human bar chart. The pupils should then decide on alternative ways that they could record the data.

Developing mathematical thinking and reasoning: the pupils are making their own decisions about the collection and representation of the data. This develops their understanding and awareness of the data handling cycle.

Recording: take photographs of the human bar chart and create a display with the alternative forms of representation that the pupils come up with.

Communicating learning: the class could prepare a presentation to give to the school council. It would be fantastic if the school actually adapted their school dinners based on the research.

Possible developments: the activity could be extended to explore other whole school issues.

Skills developed:

- answering a set of related questions by collecting, selecting and organising relevant data; drawing conclusions from their own and others' data and identifying further questions to ask.
- drawing and interpreting frequency tables, pictograms and bar line charts, with the vertical axis labelled for example in 2s, 5s, 10s, 20s or 100s and considering the effect of changing the scale on the vertical axis.

Task 10.9 Healthy and unhealthy food

Some food that you eat is healthy and some food that you eat will be unhealthy.

Cut pictures out of magazines of as many different sorts of food as you can.

Use these pictures to complete this Carroll diagram.

	Healthy food	Not healthy food
Food I like		
Food I don't like		

Target group: Y1/2/Stages 1 and 2.

Resources: laminated photos of food for the introduction; newspapers and magazines for pupils to cut out images of food (make sure you have looked through so that there are plenty of images to choose from); large versions of the Carroll diagram.

Possible starting point: create a large Carroll diagram on the whiteboard. Have a few laminated photographs of food prepared. Select pupils from the class to come up to the front and place the picture in the appropriate cell for them. Make the point that different pupils would place pictures in different cells. There is not a 'correct' answer.

Representing and recording the problem: use large versions (A3 paper if possible) of the Carroll diagram so that pupils can physically place the photographs in position. An alternative is to use masking tape to create very large Carroll diagrams on the floor. You may want to take photographs of the completed Carroll diagrams.

Developing mathematical thinking and reasoning: pupils should work in small groups both to find the images and to sort the images. The discussion about where to place the image will allow them to understand how Carroll diagrams are used to sort data.

Communicating learning: each group should present their results. Encourage the different groups to notice the similarities and differences between their diagrams and encourage discussion around the differences.

Possible developments: this activity can be used for other data sets.

Skills developed:

- interpreting and constructing simple tables
- asking and answering simple questions by sorting
- asking and answering questions about totalling and comparing categorical data
- using Carroll and Venn diagrams to sort numbers or objects using one criterion; beginning to sort numbers and objects using two criteria; explaining choices using appropriate language, including 'not'.

Task 10.10 Letters in my name

How many letters are there in your name?

Create a pictogram that shows this information for your class.

If you have links with other schools see how many letters are in the children's names at other schools.

Target group: Y1/2/Stages 1 and 2.

Resources: photographs or images of the pupils; links with other schools where the pupils may have different naming patterns.

Possible starting point: this is a good activity to carry out as a whole class. It does not need to take a whole session and could be an introduction to other sorting and data collection activities such as the activities above. Start the activity by asking pupils to bring in passport-sized photographs of themselves – alternatively ask them to draw a small image which can represent themselves and to write their name underneath the image. Then ask the pupils to count the number of letters in their first name.

Then construct a human bar chart by placing numbers on the floor to represent the numbers of letters in the first name. Ask pupils to line up next to the number which represents their name.

Represent the problem: take a photograph of the human bar chart and then create a pictogram using the photographs or images. Talk about the two ways of representing the data. Use discussion partners to talk about the advantages and disadvantages of the two representations.

Developing mathematical thinking and reasoning: still using discussion pairs the pupils should talk about things that they notice from the data. Is there anything that surprises them?

Communicating learning: the pupils can share the facts that they noticed in the data. Each pair should also pose a further question that can be asked as a result of working with this data.

Recording: the photograph of the human bar chart and the pictogram can be displayed and annotated with the 'facts' that the pupils have noticed, together with the further questions that they want to ask.

Possible developments: make links with a school with a contrasting catchment area to yours and ask them to share their data with you. It would be great if this could be a school in another country. You can also work on the questions that have been raised by the pupils at the end of the session.

Skills developed:

- interpreting and constructing simple pictograms, tally charts, block diagrams and simple tables
- asking and answering simple questions by counting the number of objects in a category and sorting categories by quantity
- asking and answering questions about totalling and comparing categorical data.

Task 10.11 Probability

Think about events that could complete these sentences.

- It is absolutely certain that ....

- There is a small possibility that ....

- It is unlikely ....

- There is a fifty–fifty chance that ....

- It is possible that ....

- It is very likely ....

- It is certain ....

Try to line these events up on a probability line.

Which do you know are correct?

Which are estimates or approximations?

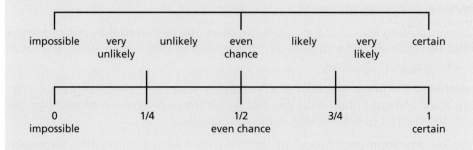

Target group: Y5/6/Stages 5 and 6.

Resources: large copy of the probability line.

Possible starting point: the activity is self-explanatory. It is better to support learners to work in all attainment groups for this activity so that the groups have a wide range of experience to draw on. You may want to ask each group to think of an event that is 'absolutely certain' to begin with and share these thoughts.

Represent the problem: use the probability number line to represent the thinking. It is helpful if pupils write the events on pieces of paper so that they can move them around on the number line whilst they agree on a probability. You could use a 'washing line' at the front of the class and ask pupils to share their events on this line. This will also facilitate discussion about the likelihood of particular events.

Developing mathematical thinking and reasoning: the discussion about the likelihood of events happening supports the development of mathematical thinking and reasoning. You should point out the difference between experimental probability (this is the ratio of an event happening to the total number of events – so you could toss a coin 100 times to see how many heads you get. It is unlikely to be exactly 50!) and theoretical probability (this would say that the probability of getting a head is 50% as there are only two possible outcomes).

Communicating learning: create a number line that the whole class can share their events on. This means that groups have to justify the decisions they have made about the probability of their events.

Possible developments: create experiments which can explore some of the probabilities that have been assigned to events.

Skills developed:

- using the language associated with probability to discuss events, to assess likelihood and risk, including those with equally likely outcomes.

Task 10.12 The great horse race

You are going to play the great horse race game. You roll two dice and move the horse forward according to the dice score.

Play the game five times. Before each game pick a horse that you think will win.

1										
2										
3										
4										
5										
6										
7										
8										
9										
10										
11										
12										

Which horses can never win?
Which horses are unlikely to win?
Which horses are most likely to win?

Explain your answers.

Target group: Year 5/6/Stages 5/6

Resources: a copy of the game board; two different coloured dice for each group.

Possible starting point: for this activity I would allow the pupils to start the activity in their all attainment groups. It is an advantage for the pupils to come to understand the different probabilities through playing the game.

Representing and the problem: pupils may choose to create a table which shows all the different scores with two dice. If they use separate columns for the two different colours of dice they will see that throwing a 1 and then a 2 is a different outcome from throwing a 2 and then a 1. They will need to represent the different outcomes in some way to see why some outcomes are more likely than others.

Developing mathematical thinking and reasoning: the three questions at the end of the task sheet are key to the development of mathematical thinking and reasoning. The pupils should discuss these questions in their groups and record their own thoughts.

Communicating learning: ask each group to share the results of the game. These can be combined so that you have data from the whole class. There should then be an extended discussion of the explanations for the questions at the end of the task sheet.

Possible developments: develop other probability experiments as in the activity above.

Skills developed:

- using the language associated with probability to discuss events, to assess likelihood and risk, including those with equally likely outcomes.

GLOSSARY

2D: Two-dimensional. Describes a shape that has length and width, but not depth. 2D shapes move so that we can see them in any orientation.

3D: Three-dimensional. Describes a shape that has length, width and depth. 3D shapes can roll, slide, build and balance.

area: The amount of space a shape takes up. Measured in units such as square millimetres, square centimetres or square kilometres, written mm², cm² or km².

array: A set of numbers or objects arranged in order, often in rows and columns.

axes: Reference lines that cross at right angles; used to locate points by their coordinates.

bar chart: Diagram that uses bars or rectangles to represent discrete data.

Carroll diagram: Diagram used to represent data in a tabular, yes/no format.

common multiples: Multiples that are shared by two or more numbers. So a common multiple of 3 and 6 is 12, as 3 and 6 are both factors of 12.

congruent shapes: Two shapes that will fit perfectly on top of each other.

continuous data: Data that has an infinite number of possible values, such as heights, weights and time.

counting on: Technique for performing simple calculations (addition, subtraction) by reference to a number line.

cube: A 3D shape with all its faces squares.

cuboid: A 3D shape with all its faces rectangles.

decimal notation: System used to express numbers and parts of numbers as multiples and sub-multiples of 10.

denominator: The lower part of a fraction, representing the number of parts into which the whole has been divided. For example, the denominator of 5/7 is 7.

directed numbers: Numbers with a plus or minus sign attached, to show whether it is a positive or negative number. So +7 means 'positive' 7 and −3 means 'negative' 3.

discrete data: Data that can be counted.

edges: The boundary lines of a 2D shape, or the straight line where two faces of a 3D shape meet.

equivalent fractions: Fractions with the same value, such as 6/8 and 3/4, or 70/100 and 7/10.

faces: The flat regions of a 3D shape.

factors: The various numbers that divide exactly into a given number.

For example, the factors of 12 are 1, 2, 3, 4, 6 and 12.

frequency table: Used to record observations of frequencies.

generalise: To make a statement that is true about a wide range of cases.

integers: Numbers that have no decimal or fractional parts; sometimes called a whole number. Can be either positive or negative. Integers should not be confused with natural numbers.

irregular shapes: Shapes with sides and angles that are different lengths and sizes.

line of symmetry: Line about which a shape with reflective symmetry can be folded so that the two halves fit exactly on top of each other.

mass: The amount of substance in an object. Not to be confused with its weight, which is the strength of the gravitational pull on the object – that is, how heavy it is.

mean: Average value, calculated by adding up all the different items of data and dividing by the total number of items.

median: The middle value of a set of data when all the data is arranged in order.

mode: The value that occurs most frequently in a set of data.

net: Two-dimensional shape that can be folded to make a three-dimensional shape.

obtuse angle: An angle between 90° and 180°.

parallel sides: Two sides that are always the same distance apart and will never meet, no matter how far

you extend them.

parallelogram: Quadrilateral with opposite sides parallel.

partitioning: Splitting a number to enable you to carry out a calculation mentally: so, for example, 24 = 2 tens and 4 units = 20 + 4.

perimeter: The distance all the way round the outside edge of a shape; measured in mm, cm or km, for example.

perpendicular: Describes the relationship between two objects – such as lines or surface – that meet at right angles (90°) to each other.

pictogram: Diagram that uses pictures of objects to represent discrete data.

polygon: Any shape with straight edges.

prime number: Number with only two factors: itself and 1.

probability: The likelihood of an event occurring.

pyramid: Solid object with a base that is a polygon, and with sides that meet at the top.

range: A measure of the spread of a set of data.

rectangle: Any quadrilateral with four sides.

rectilinear shapes: Shapes that can be split up into a series of rectangles.

reflex angles: Angles greater than 180°.

regular polygons: Polygons with all sides the same length and all angles between the sides the same; any other sort of polygon is irregular.

regular shape: Shape with all sides the same length and all interior angles the same size.

rhombus: Quadrilateral with four equal sides.

rotational symmetry: Property of a shape that looks the same after it has been rotated through less than 360°.

rounding: Reducing the number of digits in a number but keeping its value roughly the same.

specialising: Looking at specific examples in order to get started on a problem.

square: Quadrilateral with four equal sides and four right angles.

square number: The result of multiplying (squaring) a number by itself.

standard units: Units that are in common usage, such as metres, litres or kilograms, and all the derived (related) units.

surface area: Total area of all faces of a 3D shape.

symmetry: The property of a shape that is made up of identical parts facing each other or when rotated round an axis.

tally charts: Diagrams that uses sets of ticks or hash marks to represent discrete data.

Venn diagram: Diagram that uses overlapping shapes (usually circles or ellipses) to show the relationships between groups of things that share something in common.

INDEX

2D shapes 112, 119, **178**; in a bag 124, 125; dimensions and angles 129; properties of 125; recognising and naming 125; visualising 151

3D shapes 73, 89, 112, 117, 119, **178**; in a bag 124, 125; identifying from 2D representations 127; properties of 125; recognising and naming 125; recognition of 127; visualising 127, 151

20, making 78–9

100 squares 58–9, 67, 93; patterns 96–7

acute angles 115, 117, 129

addition(s) 39, 77

additions(s) 92–3

'aha' moments 111, 121

algebra 95; balances 104–5; bead strings 102–3; cats ears, calculating 100–1; Christmas crackers 108–9; goats and chickens 110–11; growing shapes 98–9; patterns in 100 square 96–7; ratio 106–7

angles: acute 115, 117, 129; equal 121; obtuse 115, 117, 129, **179**; reflex 121, 129, **179**; right 115, 117, **179**

area **178**; measurement of 136–7

arrays 62, 63, 81, 84–5, **178**

averages 157, 159, 165, 167

axes 155, 157, 159, 167, 169, **178**

balance scales 104–5, 134

bar charts 155, **178**; human 168–9

bar line charts 157, 159, 167, 169

bead strings 102–3

best value 90–1

block diagrams 173

Boaler, Professor Jo 2–3

board meetings 55

Brown, Laurinda 13

building towers 83

bunting, making 128–9

calculating 75; additions 92–3; arrays and fact families 84–5; best value purchase 90–1; checking calculations 82–3; chick peas to fill a classroom 88–9; largest product 86–7; making 20 78–9; mental methods 76–7; new facts for old 80–1

calculations, checking 82–3

Cambridge International Examinations 2, 11

capacity 132, 133, 135, 143, 147, 149, 151

car parking 31

Carroll diagrams 64, 65, 117, 160, 161, 163, 171, **178**

categorical data 171, 173

centi 133, 143

centimetres 151

cereal boxes 150–1

charts 155, 157; *see also* bar charts; bar line charts; human bar charts; tally charts

chickens 110–11

chick peas 88–9

Christmas crackers 108–9

circles 125; with nodes 109

circumference 106

classification(s) 65, 161, 163

clocks 144–5

column method 87

common multiples 73, **178**

commutativity 81

comparison, language of 149

composite rectilinear shapes 141, 151

congruent shapes 125, **178**

conservation 135

consortium 137

continuous data 155, 157, **178**

conversions 52–3

counting and understanding number 33; conversions 52–3; decimals 50–1; estimating cubes 34–5; fractions 48–9, 50–1; measuring temperature 38–9;

multiplying and dividing by 10 44–5;
number sequencing 40–1; number
track, counting on a 36–7; place value
42–3, 45; planning a party 54–5;
rounding 46–7
counting on 59, **178**
counting sticks 47, 67
cubes 19, 83, **178**; estimating 34–5;
interlocking 126–7; shapes out of
126–7; *see also* stock cube boxes
cubic units 141
cuboids 73, 89, 125, 140, 141, 151, **178**

data 154–5, 157, 158–9, 171, 173
decimal notation 45, 91, **178**
decimals: fractions and 50–1
decorating groups 55
denominators 51, **178**
diagonal 121
diagrams 155
digit cards 42, 43
digit sums 67
directed numbers 39, **178**
discrete data 155, 157, **178**
distributive law 62–3
dividing by 10 44–5
divisions 51
dominoes 26–7
doubling patterns 15

edges 125, **178**
energy bills 31
entertainment groups 55
equal angles 121
equal sides 121
equilateral triangles 121, 129
equivalence 51
equivalent fractions 49, **178**
estimating cubes 34–5
estimating skills 147
estimation 89, 91
evaluation 155
evenness 83
even numbers 21, 64, 65, 67; calculating
with 82–3
experimental probability 175

faces 125, **178**
fact families 84–5
factors 73, **178**
facts, new for old 80–1
folding and cutting 120–1
foods, healthy and unhealthy 170–1

fractions 48–9; and decimals 50–1
frequency tables 155, 157, 159, 167, 169,
179

generalisations 59, 61; algebra 97, 99
generalise 59, 63, 95, **179**
geometry 113; bunting, making 128–9;
folding and cutting 120–1; line of
symmetry 122–3; polygons 115,
116–17; shapes in a bag 124–5; shapes
out of cubes 126–7; sorting triangles
118–19; visualisation 114–15, 125, 127
goats 110–11
graphs 155
great horse race game 176–7
grid method 87
grids 16
groups: Christmas crackers 108; party
planning 55

handshake problem 109
height 149
heptagons 115, 117
human bar charts 168–9, 172, 173
hypotheses 97, 99, 121, 129

iconic representations 79
imperial units 138
instrumental understanding 8
integers 11, **179**
irregular polygons 121
irregular shapes 125, 141, 151, **179**
isometric paper 73, 127, 141
isosceles triangles 121, 129

key stage 1 10
kilo 133, 143
kite 120

largest product 86–7
length 132, 133, 147, 149
lessons: outstanding 1–2
letters in a name 172–3
line of symmetry 122–3, **179**
lower key stage 2 10–11

marketing groups 55
Mason, John 8, 111
mass 10, 132, 133, 135, 143, 147, 149, **179**
mathematical vocabulary 117, 119, 125
mean 157, 159, 164–5, 167, **179**
measurement 129, 131; appropriate units
138–9; area and perimeter 136–7;

cereal boxes 150–1; knowledge of 132–3; measuring jugs, making 142–3; more than/less than 1kg 146–7; teddy bears picnic 148–9; time, telling the 144–5; true/false/iffy statements 140–1; weight 134–5
measuring jugs 142–3
median 157, 164–5, 167, **179**
medium 159
mental addition 24–5
mental calculations 76–7
metric units 133, 139
milli 133, 143
mini olympics 156–7
mode 157, 159, 164–5, 167, **179**
modelling 19, 61
multiplication facts 101; patterns in 66–7
multiplying by 10 44–5
mystic rose 109

nets 73, 151, **179**
noticing, skill of 161, 163
number lines 41, 77, 93, 175
number sense 35
number sequences 79, 97, 99
number sequencing 40–1
number sorting 64–5, 162–3
number track, counting on a 36–7

objects: measurement of 132; volume of 132; weight of 132
obtuse angles 115, 117, 129, **179**
odd numbers 21, 64, 65, 67; calculating with 82–3
Ofsted (Office for Standards in Education, Children's Services and Skill) 1
oral reasoning 101
outstanding lessons 1–2

parallelogram 120, 121, **179**
parallel sides 121, **179**
partitioning 43, 68–9, 79, **179**; arrays 81
patterns 15, 16; algebraic, in a 100 square 96–7; bead strings 103; growing 99; in multiplication facts 66–7
peer assessment 151, 155
pentominoes 29
perimeters 73, 136–7, 141, **179**
perpendicular 121, **179**
photographs 149
picnics 148–9
pictograms 155, 157, 159, 167, 169, 173, **179**

pictorial representations 79
place value 42–3, 45, 69, 81, 87
place value cards 43, 68, 69
planning a party 54–5
polygons 115, 116–17, **179**; regular 121
presentations 73
Primary Years Programme 2
prime numbers 8, 64, 85, **179**
probability 174–5, **179**
problem solving using mathematics 2–3, 13–32; approaches 7–10; tasks 14, 18, 20, 22, 24, 26, 28, 30
product, largest 86–7
proof 16, 19, 61, 83
properties of numbers 57; distributive law 62–3; operations on a 100 square 58–9; partitioning 68–9; patterns in multiplication facts 66–7; sorting numbers 64–5; square and triangular numbers 60–1; stock cube boxes 72–3; totals 10 totals 100 70–1
proportion 107, 111
protractors 129
purchasing groups 55
puzzles 101
pyramids 125, **179**

quadrilaterals 115, 117, 119, 121

range 164–5, **179**
ratio 106–7, 111, 129
reading 166–7
rectangles 51, 125, 140, 141, 151, **179**
rectilinear shapes 137, 141, 151, **179**; composite 141, 151
recycling paper 31
reflection 8, **179**
reflective symmetry 121
reflex angles 129, **179**
refreshments groups 55
regular polygons 121, **179**
regular shapes 125, **180**
relational understanding 8
relationships 97, 107
rhombus 120, 121, **180**
right angles 115, 117
rotational symmetry 121, 122, **180**
rounding 46–7, 89, **180**

scalene triangles 121, 129
scaling problems 109
scatter diagrams 106, 107
school travel 31, 158–9

shading 49
shapes 114–15; in a bag 124–5; congruent
    125; growing 98–9; irregular 125, 141,
    151; out of cubes 126–7; regular 125;
    sorting of 160–1; *see also* 2D shapes;
    3D shapes
shelters, building 149
Skemp, Richard 8
sorting numbers 64–5, 162–3
specialising 95, **180**
spheres 125
spread, measures of 165
square centimetres 141
square metres 141, 151
square numbers 60–1, **180**
square(s) 8, 120, **180**
square units 141
standard units 135, 141, 147, 151, **180**
statistics 153; data, meaning of 154–5;
    great horse race game 176–7; healthy
    and unhealthy food 170–1; human bar
    charts 168–9; letters in a name 172–3;
    mean, median, mode and range 164–5;
    mini olympics 156–7; number sorting
    162–3; probability 174–5; reading
    166–7; school travel 158–9; shape
    sorting 160–1
stimulus sheets 65
stock cube boxes 72–3
subtraction 39, 77
surface area 73, **180**
sustainable schools 30–2
symmetry 112, 115, 117, **180**; line of
    122–3; reflective 121; rotational 121,
    122
systematic recording 137

tables 155, 171, 173
tally charts 155, 173, **180**
teddy bears picnic 148–9
temperature 147; measuring 38–9
tetrahedrons 115, 117
theoretical probability 175
thermometers 38, 39
time, telling the 144–5
Top Trumps game 132, 139
totals 10 70–1
totals 100 70–1
trapezium 120, 121
triangles 115, 117, 121, 125, 129;
    identifying and describing properties
    of 129; sorting 118–19
triangular numbers 60–1
true/false/iffy statements 140–1
'two stars and a wish' process 151, 157,
    159

unit costs 91
unit cubes 151
units of measurement 138–9
upper key stage 3 11–12

Venn diagrams 117, 161, 162–3, 171, **180**
vertical axis 157, 159, 167, 169
vertices 125
visualisation 114–15, 117, 121, 125, 127
vocabulary, mathematical 117, 119, 125
volume 85, 89, 132, 135, 149

wall displays 119
weight 132, 133, 134–5, 147, 149

Also available:

Understanding and Teaching Primary Mathematics

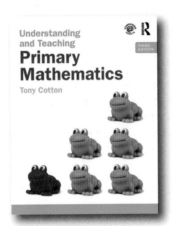

Written by an education consultant with widespread experience of teaching mathematics in the UK and internationally, *Understanding and Teaching Primary Mathematics* seamlessly combines pedagogy and subject knowledge to build confidence and equip you with all the skills and know-how you need to successfully teach mathematics to children of any age.

This third edition has been fully updated to reflect the latest research developments and initiatives in the field, as well as key changes to both the UK National Curriculum and International Baccalaureate, including a brand new chapter on 'Algebra' and a reworked focus on the early years. Extra features also include helpful call-outs to the book's revised and updated companion website, which offers a shared site with a range of resources relevant to both this book and its new companion volume, *Teaching for Mathematical Understanding*.

Stimulating, accessible and well-illustrated, with comprehensive coverage of subject knowledge and pedagogy, *Understanding and Teaching Primary Mathematics* is an essential purchase for trainee and practising teachers alike.

What the experts are saying about the book:

Once again, Tony Cotton has produced a very accessible and engaging book which will be a great support to trainee teachers from a range of teaching routes, including School Direct and Teach First. The book gives insight into a range of activities and resources which can be used in the class, providing comprehensive links to National Curriculum requirements. It supports these with an in-depth analysis of some of the issues related to the teaching of mathematics, such as subject knowledge and pedagogy. Portfolio tasks and self-audits are provided, which will help to develop and enrich practice. This book is altogether a very practical classroom support which will be an invaluable resource for those seeking to enhance their own practice.

Keith Brentnall, Senior Lecturer in Primary Mathematics, Northumbria University, UK

PB ISBN: 978-1-138-90640-2
HB ISBN: 978-1-138-90638-9
eISBN: 978-1-315-69552-5